THE *Black* PEARL NECKLACE

A MEMOIR BASED ON
THE SOUTH SEA JOURNALS
OF JOANNE JONES

KEN JONES

Copyright © 2018 Ken Jones.

All rights reserved. No part of this book may be reproduced, stored, or transmitted by any means—whether auditory, graphic, mechanical, or electronic—without written permission of the author, except in the case of brief excerpts used in critical articles and reviews. Unauthorized reproduction of any part of this work is illegal and is punishable by law.

This book is a work of non-fiction. Unless otherwise noted, the author and the publisher make no explicit guarantees as to the accuracy of the information contained in this book and in some cases, names of people and places have been altered to protect their privacy.

ISBN: 978-1-4834-8207-1 (sc)
ISBN: 978-1-4834-8205-7 (e)

Library of Congress Control Number: 2018902806

Because of the dynamic nature of the Internet, any web addresses or links contained in this book may have changed since publication and may no longer be valid. The views expressed in this work are solely those of the author and do not necessarily reflect the views of the publisher, and the publisher hereby disclaims any responsibility for them.

Any people depicted in stock imagery provided by Getty Images are models, and such images are being used for illustrative purposes only. Certain stock imagery © Getty Images.

Lulu Publishing Services rev. date: 04/13/2018

Authors Note:

This is a memoir of events beginning in 2007 that is a story of grace and courage in the face of an uncertain future. I have long wanted to share this story of *The Black Pearl Necklace* but I didn't feel able until after attending a Writers' Retreat in the spring of 2015.

At that time, I had another story in mind and with the encouragement of others at the retreat, my first effort, *Letters from the Skeleton Coast,* is now available online or and at book stores everywhere. With that experience behind me, I have now completed *The Black Pearl Necklace.* Both stories involve my former wife Joanne, a most beautiful and remarkable woman. She touched the lives of many with her laughter, her positive attitude, and her high spirit.

I believe this story, which includes Joanne's own travel journals, will not only give you an insight into her life, and possibly a look into your own life in the world to come.

Prologue

April 1, 2009

"Ring --- ring." "Ring --- ring." "Ring --- ring."

Drew was curled up on the couch in my office where he had spent the night. I had fallen asleep in my big reading chair while we were talking about Joanne and what would come next in our lives. It was seven o'clock.

"Ring --- ring."

I sat up as my son struggled over to the desk and answered the phone. As I was finally sitting in an upright position, "Jones residence." After a pause, he held out the phone for me with a quizzical look. "It's the manager of the Hilton Hotel in Auckland, New Zealand. He wants to talk with you."

I blinked to clear my head and stepped over to the desk. "Hello, this is Ken Jones."

Drew mumbled something about "anyone calling so early in the morning" and went into the kitchen to make a pot of coffee. We had a late night and were both in an unsettled state of finality. Joanne and I were married a few years after Drew's mother passed away. Over the years, he and Joanne had come to love each other very much --- and now she was also gone.

Joanne had died at seven o'clock last night. By the time the hospice workers and the funeral home personnel left with her fragile little body, it was close to midnight.

I didn't want to go back into the bedroom to spend the rest of the night there and Drew seemed to prefer the couch in my office to the guest room downstairs. We just sat in my office and talked --- small talk, stories about Joanne, and what life would be like now without her.

"Yes, my wife and I were guests of the hotel recently. No, I don't recall the exact dates but I'll check on my desk calendar. Okay, here it is --- it was February 2nd. We were there for three nights."

"Yes, we did file a missing item report. I recall going to the front desk where the clerk gave me a form to complete. I reported that a black pearl necklace was missing from our room as we prepared to check out. That was about eleven o'clock in the morning."

"No, we did not find it later. What's this all about?"

After listening for several minutes, I said, "Yes, please do --- and thank you."

After a short pause, I added, "Oh, by the way, when did you find them? I mean ---what time were they returned?"

I listened intently, "Yes, yes. Thank you very much."

During the call, Drew came back into my office and had put a steaming hot cup of coffee on my desk. He had heard the last part of my side of the conversation, and when I put the phone down, I looked at Drew as he said, "What the hell was that all about?"

I didn't reply immediately since my mind was racing. Then, after a quick calculation of the time difference between New Zealand and North Carolina, I said, "You are not going to believe what just happened."

He looked puzzled. I took the cup in both hands and after a taste of the orange flavored coffee we always kept on hand when we knew Drew was coming for a visit, "Well, let me tell you the amazing story of the black pearl necklace."

CHAPTER

SPRING, 2007

I was scheduled to have surgery to fuse two disks in my neck, one above and one below the fusion I had in 2001 resulting from a boating accident. I had put off the surgery for several years; however, now that Joanne had received a "clean bill of health" following breast cancer treatment, it was time to get it over with once and for all. I had several "second" opinions. While the recommendations were not always the same, the feeling was it needed to be done.

In the past few weeks, however, Joanne had commented about a raspy feeling in her throat. With some urging from me, she finally went to see Dr. Caserio, our family doctor here in Hendersonville. He was a good friend and familiar with Joanne's medical situation. He recommended she see a pulmonary specialist immediately to check out the underlying cause of the irritation.

Dr. Lamb, a young woman doctor, felt a little swelling in Joanne's neck and suspected an issue with her thyroid glands. She had performed a needle biopsy performed, and then sent the sample to the Pardee Hospital lab. That seemed a little extreme to me since Joanne had never had any thyroid problems in the past. When the report came back the next day from the pathologist, saying that there were breast cancer cells in her thyroid, our world stopped dead in its tracks.

The report was sent to Dr. Radford, the oncologist who had treated Joanne for the past five years. He was more than just her doctor as he was now her good friend. Radford's thought was there had not been any reports in medical journals of breast cancer cells metastasizing into the thyroid gland, however, just in case, he suggested that Dr. Sears, a well known ENT surgeon in North Carolina, remove the affected portion of the gland.

I immediately canceled my neck surgery since Joanne's issues were now of much greater concern, it took several weeks to get her procedure lined up at Mission Hospital in Asheville --- the same hospital where I had been scheduled just a few weeks earlier. During her surgery on Friday morning, I was called to the operating area to review with Dr. Seal the situation as it had developed. He had indeed removed the left portion of Joanne's thyroid, however, the pathologist on duty in the operating room had found what appeared to be breast cancer cells. Not in the thyroid, but behind the thyroid gland and attached to the wall of the trachea. He had removed as much of the affected area as possible without damaging Joanne's appearance. Based on his meetings with Joanne prior to surgery, he recommended that we stop there.

I agreed. The last thing Joanne would want was to be disfigured.

The report was faxed to Dr. Radford, late on a Friday afternoon, and he immediately went into action. A Positron Emission Tomography study, more commonly known as a PET scan, was ordered for Sunday morning. It was a difficult weekend for us following the surgery; we had to wait for the scan results, not knowing what would come next.

Dr. Radford's office called early on Monday morning and asked that we come in that afternoon. He went over the pathology report as we looked at the PET scan on his computer. It was basically an outline that looked like an X-ray of her whole body. He pointed out several small white spots in different locations on the image.

One was in the area of her surgery; however, there were others throughout her body. A scan measures intense energy or unusual emissions. As always, he went over her situation with us in very careful detail.

Cancer cells absorb more energy than normal cells and show up clearly on the scan. They are given a value from one to ten. Several of the white spots on Joanne's images registered six or seven on the scale which meant these cells were "hot --- very hot." After we talked a while longer, Joanne finally asked Dr. Radford, "What does this all mean?"

Dr. Radford reached over and took Joanne's hand. "The survival rate for someone who has breast cancer metastasized throughout her body, on average, is less than two years." He went on. "I said this was an average. Of course Joanne, we all know that you're not average."

Those words are indelibly etched in my mind.

It was a day I will never forget.

CHAPTER 2

A FEW WEEKS LATER

Dr. Radford suggested Joanne consider participating in a new drug trial which was just underway by one of the major pharmaceutical companies. The drug was being developed in connection with treatment of lymphoma and cancer of the blood cells. It had been more than twelve months since she had chemotherapy of any kind so he thought she could qualify for the program. He felt that since her breast cancer cells had metastases outside of the original area this could be a more effective treatment than traditional chemotherapy that apparently had not been completely successful in the past. He cautioned, however, that the new drug was "in trial" and had not been designed or approved for this application. There could be no assurance of success.

A request would have to be made to the company for Joanne to become involved but we all agreed to move forward. We included Joanne, Dr. Radford and me, and also Leann Noakes, her oncology nurse. During the prior five years of chemotherapy, Leann had become much more than just Joanne's nurse --- but now her good friend. Over the past few years, Leann and Joanne had spent hours together every few weeks during the treatments and were more like sisters; plus Leann was the New Drug Trial Administrator for Pardee Hospital.

The application and acceptance would take several weeks; maybe even as much as a month for final approval by the drug company. However, after all of the other treatment options were considered, it was thought to be the best plan for survival.

Without hesitation, Joanne said, "If this may help, and I can be helpful to others who are in my situation, let's get on with it."

On that day in the car on the way home from Dr. Radford's office Joanne was unusually quiet. The events of the past month had taken her from "a clean bill of health" and the highest of highs --- to a two year "death sentence" and the lowest of lows.

About half-way into the twenty minute drive home, Joanne said, "Do you remember the special brochure we received in the mail a few weeks ago from *Silversea*? You know the one about the America's Cup races in Spain --- the cruise to nowhere."

I turned to look at her.

She had a big smile on her face, "I'll check to see if they still have space available. If they do, then let's go."

She went on, "The timing is just right, we'll fly to Spain and take the new *Silversea Whisper* to Valencia to watch the races and be back in time to start my trial." After a pause, "Oh honey, it will be perfect --- the America's Cup --- it is something we have talked about doing ever since we've been married."

My mind went through the full range of emotion during the rest of the way home. I could see the excitement in her eyes as we drove along. I smiled. "That is a great idea, but let's check with Radford first, just to make sure it won't delay the treatments."

I know Dr. Radford was surprised when he received a phone call from Joanne less than an hour after leaving his office. Joanne outlined the idea. He knew Joanne well and thought it was a great plan.

"I'll schedule a new PET scan for the day after you return

from Spain and, if approved, the trial can begin the next day." Then he added, "Joanne, you are amazing."

We called the private travel agent number for *Silversea*. They did have a stateroom available so with that; our trip would begin within two weeks.

CHAPTER

3

THE 2007 AMERICA'S CUP

The flight to Spain took us through Dulles in Washington D.C. and then to London before arriving in Barcelona. We would spend the day and night there before the cruise ship arrived. Joanne, who had lived in Spain many years earlier while working for an international oil drilling company, had many sights she wanted to show me. Even though we were both tired after our long trip, nothing would do but that we take off from our water-front hotel and walk to the big open air market for which Barcelona is famous. An amazing place and we had lots of fun, but I was more interested in having dinner and getting to bed so we would be ready when the *Silversea Whisper* arrived the next day.

We had sailed on both the *Silversea Cloud* and the *Silversea Wind* on prior trips. The *Whisper*, while slightly larger, was of a similar design and provided the same personalized service which sets Silversea apart from other lines. Their well traveled clientele enjoyed the "all included" atmosphere, however, this cruise would be different. It was a "trip to nowhere" --- from Barcelona to Valencia, and back again.

Silversea Cruise Line is owned by a very wealthy Italian family who also sponsored *Luna Rossa*, the Italian challenger for the America's Cup. *Luna Rossa* was in the elimination series so the owners of the syndicate would be staying on the *Whisper*. Along with Gary Jobson, John Rousmaniere and several other well known world class sailors on board, this would be an interesting passenger list. There would be only three-hundred of us, so after a few days, we would get to know almost everyone.

Cruise companies schedule their ships to arrive in port early morning so the excited passengers can go on shore excursions while some of the departing passengers leave and new ones board during the day. Most cruisers like the idea of being in port during the day and traveling to the next destination overnight --- arriving in time for more shore excursions in the next exotic port. Joanne and I had been almost everywhere by that time so when the passengers went ashore for the day, we often just stayed on board by the pool along with the few others who "had been there and done that."

That particular cruise along the coast of Spain was only three hundred nautical miles. Since the ship would dock at the new America's Cup village in Valencia, we would be there in plenty of time for the races scheduled to begin the next day. We would have a front row seat for all of the action.

During dinner the first evening, we met sailors from all over the world. As a group, we had sailed in many venues and had traveled to many exotic locations. However, this was special and we were all excited to be on board. The medical problems at home, some three thousand miles from the Mediterranean, were washed away with the conversation of the races and sailing tactics leading up to these America's Cup final races.

Joanne had a long-time family friend from California who was now involved with Larry Ellison and the big technology company Oracle. He had developed a software company that had been acquired by Oracle for several billion dollars and was now a close friend of Mr. Ellison's. He invited us for cocktails one evening during the races on board *Midnight Sun*, Ellison's mega yacht. It would be a special treat. At the time, Ellison's boat was the largest privately owned yacht in the world.

Ellison's entry in the America's Cup, appropriately named *BMW Oracle*, and was the favorite to challenge for the oldest trophy in sports. *Alinghy*, owned by the Swiss family who were the major shareholders of a giant pharmaceutical company, had won the cup in 2003 in a hotly contested series in Auckland, New Zealand.

Because of the rapid technical advancements being made by computerized designs, the new boats for the 2007 challenge would be the most sophisticated and expensive yachts ever to compete for the America's Cup. Ellison enlisted BMW as a co-sponsor in the challenge effort. They not only had a great engineering background in designing automotive airfoils but also unlimited financial support. The cost of challenging for the America's Cup was estimated to exceed $100,000,000 --- and even Mr. Ellison could use the help.

To say there was bad blood in the America's Cup at that time would be an understatement. Normally, the defending ownership syndicate selects the date and site for the next America's Cup challenge. The *Oracle* team, which had lost in the prior series in New Zealand, spent several years in court working to get the 2007 America's Cup races into a more "friendly" environment. In a spirit of compromise, Valencia was finally selected by the Swiss owners over several other sites that had been considered. As it turned out, it was the perfect site for the challenge because of the predictable afternoon winds, its neutral location, and a deep water port for the yachts of the rich and famous that would come to the event.

The race series leading up to the ultimate event is called the Louis Vuitton Cup. In 2006, fourteen countries started this elimination process. When Joanne and I left for Spain there were only three boats still in contention to determine the challenger. *Luna Rossa*, the Italian entry; *BMW Oracle*, the American entry; and the *Emirates Team New Zealand*, the New Zealand entry funded by the Middle Eastern Airline. The defending champion, *Alinghy*, was waiting in the wings to defend the Cup.

In the final races of the Vuitton series, *Luna Rossa* and *BMW Oracle* were eliminated --- leaving only New Zealand to challenge the Swiss for the 2007 America's Cup. As we approached Valencia in the late afternoon to be ready for the final race series to begin the next day, we saw Ellison's yacht *Midnight Sun* leaving and heading out to sea. Losing is hard at any level, however, when you have spent millions to get into the America's Cup and you don't make the final races, that's really hard to accept. Mr. Ellison, who has a reputation as a fierce competitor, didn't wait to see the outcome. He took his chips and went home to compete another time, so Joanne and I missed the chance to have cocktails on *Midnight Sun*.

The owners and crew of *Luna Rossa,* along with many of the other sailors and boat owners who also did not make the final races, were on board the *Whisper* during the next two weeks --- they could not have been more gracious in defeat. We were all excited just to be there now that the America's Cup race was finally underway.

Joanne and I put away all thoughts of what was to come later.

CHAPTER 4

SUMMER 2007

Arriving back in North Carolina late in the day after the thrilling final race in which *Alinghy* and the Swiss retained the America's Cup, we reported to Dr. Radford's office the next morning.

Reality quickly set in after the wonderful diversion of the past several weeks.

Joanne had indeed been accepted into the drug trial so we checked into the hospital for a new PET scan as well as an updated blood examination. The results were very similar to the last tests. There was only a slight increase in the values of the suspected cancer cells, but at least we now had a new marker in which to measure the experimental chemotherapy, which would begin the following week.

The trials were very tightly controlled; chemotherapy on Mondays and Wednesdays, then lab and blood tests on Fridays. This schedule would continue for eight weeks. Then after a two week period, new scans would measure the results to see if there were any new hot spots or changes in the energy values.

After the first series of treatments, the scans showed a slight improvement. Dr. Radford was encouraged and recommended Joanne continue with the trial for another eight week period.

Hope was very high with the thought this could be a major breakthrough.

Joanne had lost her hair again in the process but it was no longer a concern since she had several wigs from her earlier rounds of chemo. In fact, she found a new wig store in Asheville, went shopping with her best friend Karen, and came home with several new ones. One day, she was a red head, the next, she was a platinum blonde, and another day, and she was a brunette. Fortunately, she settled on one that was much like her own hair as a medium blonde with a French twist. At least, that was what I called it and she looked great --- just like her naturally beautiful self. Except now each morning it took only fifteen seconds to do her hair rather fifteen minutes as in the past!

Life went on and she was feeling very little discomfort from the new treatments.

Joanne seemed unfazed by all of the attention --- even with four hours of chemo treatments twice a week, and lab work before a visit with Dr. Radford every Friday. We became permanent fixtures in Dr. Radford's office. Joanne looked great, was smartly dressed, and always had a big smile. Terry, the office receptionist, began to call her 'Miss Hollywood.'

If you have ever spent any time in an oncologist's office, you know it can be a very grim place. Joanne made it her mission to be cheerful and to brighten up the atmosphere. The staff welcomed her with open arms. She made friends with them all; Leann was always there, as were Deanne, Barbara, Jennifer, Kathy, and the other dedicated nurses in the office.

The next set of trials went on and our hopes were very high. Unfortunately, at the end of the second eight weeks of chemotherapy, the results were not as optimistic. More hot spots had developed and their values had increased dramatically.

After a detailed review of the options, it was decided to end the trials and begin treatment with the traditional chemo chemicals which had proven to be only partially effective in the past; the long term results were now in doubt. There was a two-week waiting period before the traditional chemotherapy could begin so that the trial chemicals could be completely absorbed in her body.

It was in early November by that time. Joy and Pete, our old college friends who lived in Houston, were planning a ten day cruise of the Mexican Riviera on *Holland America* which included a side trip to the Copper Canyon in Mexico --- the Grand Canyon with a Spanish accent. That was something we had not done before and we decided to go along at the last minute.

Off we went to San Diego. The ship, the *Ryandam,* while larger than the *Silversea* or *Crystal* ships we normally preferred, had just come out of dry dock; and to our surprise, the ship and the accommodations were great. We all had a wonderful time. While in Mazatlan, Joanne took a day trip that included a zip-line traverse through a rain forest while I had a chance to sail in a match race on one of the older twelve meter America's Cup boats from the 1980s.

Something remarkable happened off the coast of Mexico while the four of us were sitting near the pool shortly after breakfast. Over the past few days, we had noticed a young couple who appeared to be by themselves and always looked very unhappy. She was wearing a baseball cap, and it seemed obvious that she had lost her hair --- probably from chemotherapy.

Joanne went over to them and engaged them in a conversation as we watched from a distance. All of a sudden, Joanne reached up and took off her hair. As she stood there --- the wig in her hands and a big smile on her face, the young couple seemed shocked. Slowly the young woman got up and took off her baseball cap. There were these two women, who had never met, standing there "naked as a jaybird." They began to laugh and then hugged --- and for the next hour, they spent time in a zone that only people with cancer understand.

The young couple was a brother and sister from New Orleans. Their parents had provided the cruise to try to give their daughter some diversion and encouragement. The hour with Joanne made all the difference in her outlook, and they became good friends and shared their private thoughts over the next week.

CHAPTER

THE COUNTDOWN BEGINS

The new year began with a revised treatment plan: chemotherapy every three weeks in Dr. Radford's office, and lab work the fourth week. The new chemo cocktail began to have a dramatic effect on her red blood count, and Joanne also had transfusions once a month at Pardee Hospital. Everywhere we went, she made friends with the staff and they became an extension of our family. As this pattern continued, month after month, and several more PET scans later, no one would have guessed Joanne's actual situation. She was now in a medical countdown --- with less than a year to live.

During one of her chemotherapy sessions, Joanne shared with Leann that there were three things she wanted to do before she was gone. Number one was: to have another football season. She loved football and the San Francisco 49ers; however, I always said it was really those big guys in tight pants who were her real interest. Number two was: to be able to dress up one more time like an antebellum lady for the Historic Flat Rock Tour of Homes. And number three was: to take one more cruise --- this time around the world.

Well, football season came and went with the 49ers losing more games than they won but that didn't seem to matter to

Joanne. We watched the TV game each Sunday afternoon, and Chinese takeout was always part of the weekend routine.

As to the tour of homes, she and her pals did get their *Gone with the Wind* dresses from the costume shop in Atlanta and again they had a great time showing the historic homes to the visitors who came to Flat Rock for the day.

Our little village of Flat Rock has been historically referred to as "little Charleston in the mountains." Before the Civil War, plantation owners and wealthy bankers from Charleston and Savannah came to the area to escape the heat and disease of the coastal communities and the low- country. They built their summer homes and shared a grand life on the scale of Newport, Rhode Island. This period came to an end as slavery was abolished and the low cost of plantation labor was over. Today, many of these estates have been broken up by real estate development. A few of stately old homes are still in existence, however, and attract thousands of visitors here for an annual tour to benefit local charities.

As it turned out, Joanne's dress that year was cut pretty low in the front and exposed the chemo port that had been put into her chest for the repeated treatments. Not to be denied, she attached a magnolia blossom over the port with a Velcro strip and she looked great. In fact, all of the ladies looked grand and were the real highlight of the 2008 tour of homes.

By the middle of December, the PET scans continued to show that the cancer cells were spreading rapidly. In spite of changing the chemical mixture several times during the year, Joanne was losing the battle. We had reached another decision point. Change the chemicals one more time to an even more toxic mixture with the debilitating results, or discontinue the treatment and let nature take its course.

For a few months, the treatments had been extracting a heavy price and the thought of spending her final days in a hospital bed was not an attractive option for her. With the countdown at about three months, she decided on her third wish: the final cruise.

The *Regent Seven Seas Cruises* had an 'around-the-world-trip' on the *Seven Seas Voyager* departing from Long Beach in early January that would spend a month in the South Pacific, a month in Asia and the Middle East, and then a month in the Mediterranean before transiting back to the United States. Ninety days in all --- we would go as far as Joanne could go.

The cruise line was wonderful when I explained our situation. They left the option to us. We could depart the ship whenever we felt it best but the stateroom would be available for the full journey. Things were now moving fast. What to pack for thirty days --- maybe more --- was her real concern. We had been on twenty-five or more cruises in the past and had our cruise essentials pretty well organized; however, this was different because we didn't know what would happen or how long the trip could last.

Joanne was really a 'junk yard dog' when it came to jewelry. She loved bling! She had all sorts of jewelry but she shared with me that there was one more thing she wanted: a black pearl necklace. It was not something you could buy at any jewelry store; but "real black pearls" from the South Pacific. Those found in the area around Tahiti were considered the most beautiful of all natural pearls and had mystical qualities. That would become an important quest of her final cruise.

Finding the perfect black pearls for a necklace, which she could leave for Drew's lovely daughter as her legacy, became her priority. She would wear them each day, and then when she was gone, they would pass to Mae and the next generation. Not just any pearls --- but the perfect black pearl necklace.

I found a new service that would pick up our luggage at our front door and deliver it directly to either our departure hotel or to the cruise ship itself. This way, we would not have to take the luggage with us through the airports --- the amount of luggage would not be a problem. So rather than be concerned about what to take, I told Joanne to pack anything she wanted. "We have enough suitcases for everything we own. For this one time, don't worry about what to wear."

CHAPTER

THE LAST CRUISE

Joanne wanted to write a daily journal of our trip to share with our friends and family. I had an old HP laptop, which probably weighed about ten pounds, so we took that along on the trip. It was a means of communication that proved invaluable before this journey was over. Dr. Radford had written a special medical protocol, which we downloaded to the computer, to give to the medical personnel on board the ship information that could be helpful should Joanne have real difficulty before we returned home.

We arrived in Long Beach a few days day before departure. We had lunch and dinner with several of her California friends. Then, much to our surprise, Mary and Bill, who live in Seattle, flew in for the sendoff. Mary and Joanne were longtime friends from high school and in recent years, we had shared several special, private issues together. Joanne appeared as if nothing was happening. She was excited, happy, smiling and beautiful as always. I am sure Bill and Mary would agree.

The day we boarded the *Seven Seas Voyager*, I found a porter to take our luggage from the hotel to our stateroom --- seven suitcases in all. After the boarding process, we settled into our suite for what would come next. Since most of the time on this cruise would be at sea, we selected a suite on the stern with a large veranda and two comfortable reclining deck chairs so that we could enjoy the open ocean view. This way we would see the ship's wake and where we had been rather than where we were going. It was terrific --- one of the best cruise experiences of our many trips.

She started writing email reports on January 13, the evening after our departure. At first, they were to just a few good friends; however, as the word spread about her reports, the mailing list grew each day. By the time she wrote her last journal --- a month later --- more than seventy-five friends receiving the daily emails.

A positive person, facing the end of life, sharing her love and enthusiasm with her family and friends in a manner that was truly Joanne. I believe you will see what I mean.

Joanne had her own language. Here are her emails --- Joanne's South Sea Journals --- unchanged and unedited, just as they were written and without benefit of hindsight --- or spell check. I'll interrupt her journals from time to time to report on how she was feeling as the trip went along and share my thoughts with some personal comments.

Then, in the short, final part of this little book, I'll explain in more detail what other events developed as the journey neared completion. I think you will agree that it is important to share her journals.

CHAPTER 7

REGENT SOUTH PACIFIC JOURNAL #1

I now begin to share our South Pacific odyssey with you as installment #1 of the Journal.

For those of you with handy navigational charts, we are currently at 27°44' 02"N 121° 04' 23W reveling in cloudless skies on a mill pond surface of the passive Pacific Ocean.

But I shall quickly digress for a moment as to all that has led up to this magical moment. Though flying to me now is one the most barbaric/masochistic exercises, our flights from Greenville to LAX actually departed and arrived on time – however, we did have a ridiculously mad dash in ATL because our commuter flight was delayed with people stuffing their belongings in the overhead bins. Then once on the way to LAX, we had to purchase a "mystery" meal --- what ever happened to the good old days when people dressed to travel and the onboard service was gracious. I just can't help but compare the olden days of glamorous flying to today's "Greyhound bus" ambience!

Having left the frigid temps of Flat Rock, we arrived to practically a nirvana in LAX: 70 plus degrees, nary a cloud and nary a suggestion of smog – the visibility was extraordinary! Our transportation was waiting (similar to a "Liz Taylor entourage") - and off we dashed for the 25 mile drive south to Long Beach and our hotel. Our room faced the Long Beach harbor, the permanently moored *Queen Mary I* cruise terminal, variety of marinas and the sunsets!! The luggage that we sent earlier (including a monstrous one we affectionately refer to as "Renaldo") was waiting for us at the hotel ... so our "stuff" added up to 7 suitcases ... Isn't that an entourage??!!!

As I had lived in the Los Angeles area for 20+ years, wonderful treasured friends drove down from both Ventura and LAX for lunch at a notable restaurant, Tract's (owned by one of those celebrity California chefs ... though this is now a "chef-ette"). Terrific innovative décor with terrific innovative cuisine! It was wonderful to reconnect, not having seen each other for many years.

Then that same afternoon we were blessed with a joyous surprise in that spectacular long time friends (high school days) showed up at the hotel to wish us Bon Voyage (they live in Seattle, but were attending meetings in Laguna Beach. "Emotional overload" doesn't begin to convey our state of mind – absolute unmitigated joy and sheer happiness to comprehend that all this goodness was actually unfolding!

The four of us savored yet another superb meal at '555' – one of those dark woody-type steak bistros ... fabulous!

Now it is THE day of sailing (13th January) – with breakfast under our belt – and hugs of "at" (never good-by) we bid farewell to our pals – found a spot to wedge ourselves in among the suitcases of the car taking us to Pier 93 and the exquisite, welcoming Regent Seven Seas Voyager. Again, the day was breathtaking: cloudless skies and the visibility from the shore allowed us to see the San Gabriel Mountains with snow-capped peaks (about 75 miles away).

At this point I could use every superlative and/or adjective in the dictionary

To describe our brief experience thus far. The ship has literally just come back into service after dry dock and shines literally like a new penny: freshly painted; all staterooms and public areas completely refurbished – and it's quiet and understated elegance. Ken and I have a saying: "E but not O" – elegant, but not ostentatious. Our stateroom with oversized verandah frames the straight and true wake as we revel in the "crossing" from LAX to Nuku Hiva.

We have lecturers to educate us in this history of these islands; the food onboard is world class (does it sound like eating is an important pastime – HELLO); service is impressive …. It's all quite surreal and everything and more that we envisioned.

Tonight is our first formal evening – with the Captain schmoozing with his "minions". In not quite 24 hrs we've met an array of interesting and charming people – this whole event is a home run!

As we have 5 more days at sea before we see land again. I will continue to discuss our "straight wake," the food (what else), the vastness of the Pacific Ocean, and the extraordinary weather that has graced us so far.

We are deliriously happy; feel terrific; and savor the fact that we're on the 'bounding main' with an array of new and unusual sights and experiences just 'round the bend!

We send our love,
Tandalaya & Capt. Cook (aka Joanne and Ken)

CHAPTER

REGENT SOUTH PACIFIC JOURNAL #2

As I forewarned, the scintillating news from our days at sea may be a bit brief ... because we're at sea. As a note, we have NOT seen another vessel; the sea continues to be like a mill pond – however, we have been advised that we're entering an "occluded weather front". We have no clue what that means, but after cocktails and dinner, we'll lash ourselves to something permanent, just in case.

It has, nevertheless, been a delightful day in that Terry Waite is a guest on board ... do you remember he was a hostage in Lebanon 1,500+ days, 3 years of which was solitary confinement. We didn't quite understand the choice of a hostage expert enroute to the South Pacific ... but he is exquisite. Huge man – easily 6'5"; speaks brilliantly; and the information he's imparting is spellbinding, contemporary and important.

Additionally, much to Ken's ebullience (great word ...) the Bridge was open so we ran, not strolled, to deck 10 and the inspection. The irony is that Ken currently is reading about Magellan, in the 1500's, searching for the strait named after him. To witness the Bridge of a 21st century vessel in comparison to the hardships of Magellan and his boys is stunning. Obviously, everything is computerized with nary a huge ship's wheel in sight – it's "joy sticks", levers and a helm "wheel" that is about the size of a child's toy car. This ship does not have a rudder nor stationary propellers, but rather two enormous steering pods with propellers that serve as rudders, thrusters and propulsion. Fascinating stuff – and Ken was in total rapture!

Last night, first formal event, Capt. Dag hosted a cocktail party wherein he introduced the executive crew and information about the ship and itinerary. Again, he's terribly attractive and looks about 30 – though we now know he's more mature, 'cuz he whipped out his glasses to read the names of his staff.

I must share this with you in that we have a gay duo onboard who are Liberace reincarnate! Their outfits and accessories last night were beyond over-the-top: vibrant brocade jackets bound with bright velvet and jewelry that would have weighed down an elephant. And, we subsequently learned, from a passenger, who has sailed with them before, that the 'bling' is the real deal … an emerald ring, alone, that was bigger than a big postage stamp … an was only one minor item. I thought it a bit overdone, personally, but made a nice statement!

The food is absolutely amazing and stunning presentation. Tonight we're going to one of the specialty restaurants, "Signatures", and I'll give a full culinary report in journal #3. As to service, here's an example of panache personified: one of the women at our table had forgotten her glasses … so instantly the waiter appeared with a "presentation box" containing about 20 pairs of glasses of different strengths. We all exclaimed what an elegant touch!

We all realize there is really no such thing as "perfection" – but I will firmly state that what we are experiencing is damn close and it's heaven.

We send our love from a spot in the Pacific – and, oh by the way, we've been advised that the ocean depth is somewhere around

13,000 ft – and is so deep it doesn't register on the fathometer at the Bridge. I just felt I had to tell you that ... mention it at your next cocktail party.

Joanne & Ken

CHAPTER

9

REGENT SOUTH PACIFIC JOURNAL #3

The sailors of yore had no idea where they were going and what to expect at whatever happened to be the "destination" …. the Pacific is a huge body of water. The same is true for the cast of characters onboard this ship …an astounding number of people in wheelchairs; those of an "advanced age" – yet balanced with younger people … the latter of which I include Ken and moi. We have a 'perfect' English couple in the suite next to us … probably in their 80's and he's disheveled with food spots on his clothes, hair growing out of his ears … and he thinks I'm a French model …. works for me!!!

Longitude 11 deg 09" 18' N / Latitude 129 deg 52" 12' W Heading …. Still, 207 deg!!

Its 10:00 PM (wherever we are) … and, guess what: we're at sea – and about 800 miles from the equator. The "occluded front" translated to leaden skies and rain – yet the sea is as calm as a mill pond. As the day unfolded, the skies cleared, the temperature rose to the low 70's – the water is a glorious "lapis lazuli" blue and the development of clouds promised a breathtaking sunset.

Obviously, meal times translates to a "Pavlov dog" event and this morning we thought we'd revel in breakfast on our verandah, but rain precluded that ... so a divine breakfast inside ... such a hardship!

We found a lovely 'cranny' and read ... but by the same token ... take advantage of the circular promenade deck and actually walk a brisk mile – easing the guilt of savoring a gorgeous dessert(s)!! The food and presentation thereof simply dazzles one's culinary desires... and probably waistlines ... but who's to care!

Of the six hundred passengers on board, 250 are circumnavigating the globe. We've now met many of them representing all ages and majority from Florida or the East Coast. Our neighbor (a single man ... NOT a George Clooney look-alike) has been on seven around the world trips and is hosting a cocktail party for the entire ship tomorrow night ... gosh, he beat us to it!

The ship also hosts a "block party" where at 5:45 PM we all emerge from our staterooms and are served wine and canapés while the captain and his executive staff visits each deck ... a fabulous concept. After the excitement of the event, the interior of the ship returned to be so quiet, we would have never known we had neighbors.

One of the South Pacific lecturers talked about Bora Bora with photos and it is so phenomenally beautiful we anxiously wait seeing it in person.

At the beginning of this journal #3, I talked about the clouds and the expectation of a magnificent sunset and the result was majestic. I must cull my photos as I have zillions of shots, but it is nature and God creating such grandeur. We even saw birds (where they 'rest' is a mystery because we're literally thousands of miles from land) plus flying fish.

We fully appreciate what we're experiencing .... totally removed from the rigors and stress of the 21st century madness and uncertainty .... and can empathize with the intrepid sailors of yore. We enjoyed an elegant Italian din/din with a Turkish waiter and with my remembrance of saying "thank you" in Turkish – we have bonded!

I end tonight underscoring how fulfilling and energizing this voyage is ... and we haven't even had our first landfall. We are in the lap of luxury and following all of your advice .... reveling in every single second ... we send our love from somewhere in the Pacific and heading south to the Equator.

Joanne & Ken

P.S. Sorry for the momentary delay in transmitting #3, but satellite connections can be crotchety.

CHAPTER

10

REGENT SOUTH PACIFIC JOURNAL #4

Latitude 6 deg 55' 38" N Longitude 132 deg 00' 06" W
Heading: 207.2 deg (still the same since departing LAX)

Hi! –guess what ... we're at sea!!! Temperature is now in the mid/high 70's and we had more rain today ... but the Pacific continues to be as serene as a mill pond. Sometimes we don't even have the sense that we're at sea other than the lovely vibration of the engines – sort of like the days of yore when one put 25¢ in the motel machine that made the mattress "vibrate".

The activities of the day were another lecture by Terry Waite and his mind-boggling and death-defying experiences as a hostage envoy in the unstable Middle East. He is a captivating speaker – and sharing his multiple terrifying experiences with "hostage takers" and the revolutionary guard makes one's hair stand on end – but his training and abilities in understanding every hostile situation is remarkable and he should be canonized .... he's already been knighted and received other commendations from Liz II – but St. Terry is certainly appropriate.

We also have another fascinating lecturer whose expertise is South Pacific history- what to see, do, etc. I simply have to share this moment in that during his talk, with photographic slides, this elderly woman (obviously oblivious to the presentation) was intent in sitting in the front row …. trundled down a side aisle wherein she walked in front of the speaker and the projector – made a huge fuss in settling into her seat – and everyone in the audience, and certainly the speaker, were aghast – then twitters of laughter spread throughout the audience. The non compus mentis lady had no clue as to the commotion she had caused. Ahhhh, to be "senior" and eccentric. I'm working very hard on achieving the status!!

Not much of a sunset this evening due to the rainy weather (my camera welcomed the inactivity). Evenings and dinner evolve into memorable serendipitous gatherings of new acquaintances – tonight being no exception. Everyone we've met in the past 4 days are wonderful, interesting, open and the couple we dined with this evening are traveling 'round the world … she's a PhD in linguistics and he looks like a line-backer from some NFL team and could/should be a stand-up comedian. Scintillating, to be sure!!

Tomorrow we cross the Equator (WOW!) and there will be a celebration onboard as we do so…. something like tossing people overboard… or possibly Mai Tai's … hopefully it's the latter! Our first landfall is Nuku Hiva in the Marquesas Islands on Tuesday the 20th. Trust me, our "crossing" has not been even remotely akin to "Two Years Before The Mast" …… just a splash more of Cabernet as opposed to hard tack and lashed to the yardarm!

With all the lectures detailing the history and glories of the islands we're about to visit, we're primed to experience the pristine and dazzling geography of these prized Pacific jewels.

We're off to the 'feathers' – lulled into the Land of Nod by the motion of the ship and the comforting sound of the engines.

Sending our love,
Joanne & Ken

CHAPTER

11

REGENT SOUTH PACIFIC JOURNAL #5

Latitude 00 deg 00' 00" S Longitude 135 deg 27' 50" W Temperature 75 deg

Yes, we're still at sea ... but this has been a banner day! As you'll note by the Latitude (00,00,00), we crossed the Equator at 3:15 PM wherever we are in whatever time zone. The event was acknowledged with frivolity, frippery (a new British word we've learned that relates to nonsense, banality, inanity) and great ceremony!

We greeted this day with tropical splendor: brilliant sun and skies; the ocean a rich cobalt blue and the froth of the wake created the most amazing hues of blues from creamy white to aquamarine blue – and it's 75 deg!!!

I'm proud to advise that I arose early enough to enjoy breakfast in a public venue – then those passengers who had not crossed by Equator by ship were treated to a Bloody Mary reception prior to lunch – then at 1:00 PM we were entertained by "King Neptune" and the theatrical crew to a spectacular ceremony of crossing the much heralded horizontal meridian!! Terry Waite assumed the role of King Neptune ... and with his profound professional career, he assumed the role with great gusto and has enchanted the ship's complement with his humor and stature. The "eye candy" captain attends all of these social events so we're not really sure when he actually "captains", but since we've been on the same heading (207°) for 2,000+ miles, this has not been a challenging navigational endeavor. It's a bit like driving from Chicago to LAX without making one single turn in the road!!

There are two specialty restaurants onboard and tonight we dined at "Prime 7" that is steak, lobster and other seafood delicacies. The décor, service and food dazzle the senses and both of us will probably be rolled off the ship like barrels. I actually savored a Maine lobster ... that somehow made the "voyage" from Penobscot Bay to the Equator – and it was decadent.

Tuesday, we trundle into Nuku Hiva and we've enjoyed a number of lectures that detail the history and majesty of these islands and we're primed to experience the extraordinary pristine beauty of these Polynesian islands. (A bit of "Funk & Wagnall" info for you: "Poly" is Greek for many; and "nesia" is Greek for a bunch of islands). You may now dismiss that tidbit or insert it into the conversation and your next cocktail party!

To think we've been at sea for 6 days and already we're devoted to this cruise; the people we've met; everything about the ship and service; and we've yet to make landfall.

As the ship's satellite didn't register with today's NFL games, we have no idea who's playing in the Super Bowl ... instead we captured sunburn (I haven't been sunburned in a zillion years and it feels delicious); and simply reveling in the vastness and majesty of the Pacific Ocean and all its nuances. To think we've traveled from LAX to Nuku Hiva (almost 3,000 miles) in 6+ days at +/- 17 knots .... And in those capricious sailing days – the same voyage would have taken months and hitting the destination was always rather vague.

Thank you for the Flat Rock report that the temperature is 9° - good grief, that has to be record breaking ... and to think we've *abandoned you and thriving in 75+ deg temps – heading for "the Second Garden of Eden" as Europe referred to the South Pacific in the 19th century.*

We send our love, Joanne & Ken (both slightly "pink" from the tropical sun)

CHAPTER

12

REGENT SOUTH PACIFIC JOURNAL #6

Latitude 7° 39' 50" S Longitude 139° 17' 38 W
Heading 207° (same since Los Angeles) Temp 80 deg – humidity 91%
Hi Ho everyone –

Yes, we're still on the briny, BUT we're on the cusp of our first landfall tomorrow –
Nuku Hiva in the Marquesas Islands – having had a crossing of 6+ days – in grand and glorious luxury. I did, however, omit an observation in yesterday's #5 journal entry in that I had rather expected some sort of "interstate sign" bobbing on a buoy announcing: "Welcome to the southern hemisphere – you have just crossed the Equator – have a nice day – and remember to keep your seat belts fastened." Instead, we watched the "count down" on our TV (sort of like the "ball" on New Year's Eve in NYC) wherein the Latitude deceased to 0 00 00 as we actually crossed this historical global dividing line.
Today was another lecture by Terry Waite which was mesmerizing as he shared the beginning of his 4+year captivity that began in Beirut. He was a humanitarian negotiator – not political nor religious – though he was an employee of the

Archbishop of Canterbury. Through a brief meeting with Oliver North – and the subsequent revelation of the Iran/Contra affair (of which Terry had no knowledge) his voracity as a negotiator was severely comprised ... and while home in the UK ... he made the decision that in order to reestablish his integrity and value of his word, he must return to Beirut. He did – and that's when he was "kidnapped" (against the vow of his "revolutionary guard" that he would be safe) and imprisoned.

Not exactly what one would expect on a South Pacific itinerary – but captivating and thoroughly engrossing. He's an imposing man with many personality facets and has endeared everyone who's been to his lectures and met him in person.

Back to the southern hemisphere: another glorious day on the bounding main ... even the officers have commented on what a calm and lovely 'crossing' we've enjoyed ... serene seas and majestic sunsets. You'll note the conspicuous absence of my impression of sunrises .... I don't "do" them .... but cocktails and sunsets are my forte!!

Tomorrow (20 January) we'll be on deck at 7:00 AM to experience a small island coming into view; the delight of landfall (a la Capt. Cook and the sailors of the 16th, 17th, 18th and 19th centuries). So, journal entry #7 will have all sorts of impressions relating to Nuku Hiva.

We are blissfully happy: enjoying the sumptuousness of this wonderful vessel and crew; gourmet meals; enlightening lecturers. Now we're going to experience the beauty of these treasured island jewels!

Our love, Joanne & Ken

CHAPTER

13

REGENT SOUTH PACIFIC JOURNAL # 7 & 8

Latitude 13 deg 49' 41" S Longitude 145 deg 53' 37W
Heading 230 deg and Temp 82 Deg
Hi Ho Everyone:

I'm combining Journal Entries #7 & #8 because yesterday was madcap and today is sedentary. I was up at 6:30 AM (I wouldn't even do that for George Clooney) ensuring that I'd be on deck as the island of Nuku Hiva came into view. I would rather have enjoyed being a sailor of yore, perched high in the riggings, shouting "land ho" after traversing almost 3,000 miles of open ocean – grog and other creature comforts lying just ahead….maybe…but at least land and solid footing.

To think that a highly crowded and seemingly world changing event was occurring in Washington DC on the 20th, we were embraced by the sheer simplicity of lovely people, exquisite day, thriving in the unspoiled majesty of a South Pacific island, literally thousands of miles from its nearest neighbor. We were treated to an interesting "festival" that included native crafts, local food, dancing, singing – and an exchange of many cultures that involved endless smiles because the Marquesans speak odd French – so between smiles and lots of gesturing, we "communicated." It's a big island (relative to South Pacific islands) yet only a dot of its territory is populated – about 2,000 people. Surprising enough (and a bit disappointing actually) the inhabitants did have cell phones and we used an ATM. Who they're talking to is a question – maybe the person standing next to them – and the ATM was instant.

The highlight of the festival was the dance of the warriors ... 10 young men that looked like NFL linebackers scantily (and I do mean <u>scantily</u>) clad in a leaf loin 'cover', leaf decorations around their knees and upper arms (the Cruise decorator did confirm they were wearing thongs as many of the elderly women seemed to be developing some sort of heart palpitations!!) Anyway, the dance was very Maori in style: lots of drum beating; fearsome loud grunting; and amazingly athletic choreography .... The original intent of terrifying their enemies (the "dance" certainly got everyone's attention – maybe not "terrified" but the gyrating, muscular bodies had an appeal). It obviously worked because they lived peacefully and happily for thousands of years ... until the explorers discovered them, followed by the wretched missionaries... but that's a 3-martini saga.

The food was all quite "mysterious" and though a number of people attacked the buffet line ... neither Ken nor I (particularly moi) wanted to risk some equally "mysterious" reaction to the cuisine – however, there was breadfruit, coconut, plantains – but the meat and fish didn't seem to have enjoyed much time over a blazing fire and wasn't very appealing looking.

After the festival we walked along the harbor breakfront and inhaled the endless fragrance of the all the blooming flora, i.e., plumeria, frangipani trees, hibiscus – and endless other varieties. We were surprised by the number of brand new cars, mainly Toyota, Nissan, Honda – and big cars! What's the price of gas? And all were 4-wheel drive! Trust me, the road system is capricious at best, partly paved, partly rutted, etc. After this rather rigorous walk (probably a couple of miles and it was hot), we boarded the tender and were deposited at the 'mother ship' in time for the 1600 hr departure.

This ship has a 21st century propulsion system, individual movable guidance pods rather than a stationary rudder with fixed propellers – the ship spun 180 degrees turning on the proverbially dime. Amazing stuff.

Being in the stern, we sunk into our verandah lounges and watched Nuku Hiva gradually disappear into the horizon.... remarking with awe at the totally unspoiled island and trying to imagine the tremendous volcanic upheaval that formed it!!

We're now enroute to Tahiti and tonight is formal – since we've had all day to be sedentary. During this day on the bounding main (which has not had a remote semblance of "bounding" as the sea continues to a mill pond – sometimes we don't even know we're moving except for the delicious subtle vibration of the engines under us) we did, however, have the final (*) lecture by Terry Waite and how and when he was released from captivity. What he endured for those 3+ years in solitary confinement (no sunlight or contact with the outside world) – always in a state of uncertainly is a testament to the human spirit, hope and determination. He shared many profound thoughts, personal anxieties and life's lessons during this ordeal --- many that I have taken to my heart relative to my situation. (*) This will NOT be his final lecture as the audience wants him back for an hour of Q&A, so the Voyager scheduling staff must find that hour somewhere.

Today, our mindless day has been enhanced by yet another day-in-paradise .... What does one do: eat, read, nap, eat ...and in about an hour we're going to see "Sadie Thompson" with Rita Hayworth and Jose Ferrer. Another one of the guest speakers is an Englishman who has been London newspaper reporter on the theatre – literally around the world – and he has selected movies with South Pacific locations/plots. The original "Mutiny on the Bounty" (with Charles Laughton and Clark Gable) has been shown, so tonight we'll become mesmerized by Rita!

Tomorrow we dock (rather than anchor) at Papeete for two nights. We plan to roam around; examine black pearls; then have schnapps at the Inter-Continental wherein sunset over the island of Moorea is reputed to be the most spectacular show on the planet. We'll let you know. Then it's Moorea where we will be looking for my special black pearl necklace for Mae. We're also planning an off-road photographic journey (with a professional photographer – and only two other couples) – then Bora Bora! (There's a special person in our world who "needs" to experience Bora Bora, so the entire visit will be dedicated to him!)

Everything continues to far exceed our wildest expectations – everything!!! Oh, one last note – even with sunscreen, hats and all the anti-sun paraphernalia, I've still garnered a little burn and it feels wonderful! I'm not quite at the "bronze goddess" state, but I don't look like Casper the Ghost!

We send our love from the Lat/Lon as detailed above.
Joanne & Ken

CHAPTER 14

JANUARY 21, 2009

We had been underway for almost ten days before I began see little changes in Joanne's daily routine. She was doing remarkably well; however, never an early morning person, she began to sleep a little longer each day. On several occasions, we even skipped breakfast in exchange for a cup of coffee served by the room butler.

When on cruises before, we seldom missed a meal so was it important to work off the extra calories. Our routine was to walk several laps around the ship mid-morning and again in the late afternoon. That was our excuse to end up at the pool side bar for quick refreshment before changing for dinner,

On this trip, however, we often skipped the morning walk. I had also noticed that Joanne's balance was becoming an issue. On several occasions, she seemed to stumble and needed to hold on the railing. She would just smile and say, "Oh, it must have been just a little bump in the ocean," and we would continue on our way.

During the quiet of one evening after leaving Nuku Hiva, we were sitting on the veranda of our stateroom. I mentioned to her that I knew she was looking for a black pearl necklace and that the jewelry shop on the main deck had just changed their window display with a beautiful large black pearl necklace as the center piece. She turned and smiled, "Maybe you don't understand. It is not the necklace --- you can buy them at most any store --- it is where they come from that is important to me."

After a few minutes, she asked if I had ever heard any of the legends about black pearls. I shook my head so she went on. "You do know that natural black pearls are very, very rare and only come from the islands around Tahiti?" She paused, "Legend has it they have a mysterious aura around them --- and have special healing powers." Then she smiled, "Here in Polynesia, they believe that God came to earth on a rainbow to give a black pearl to Princess Bora Bora as a symbol of his love. Many still believe that giving a black pearl to someone, it represents eternal life." Then she added, "In a Chinese legend, the black pearl is the symbol for infinite wisdom and truth. They were formed as the eyes of the all- powerful dragons."

I looked at her, "You do have a vivid imagination and read a lot of books, but I thought you were really into Russian history and the Czars. Where does all of this about black pearls come from?"

"Oh, there are so many legends. Another is that when Adam and Eve shed tears, they created a lake of pearls. The white pearls were formed by the tears of Eve, while the black pearls came from Adam's tears. Since men cry less than women, this explains why black pearls are so rare compared to the white ones."

I didn't say anything for a few minutes. "Well, I don't know about that one because I'm tearing up now when I hear you say things like that, but I do shed tears when I hear the 'Star Spangled Banner' played on the Fourth of July or when the jet planes buzz the stadium to start the Army Navy football game --- things like that." After wiping away a tear, I added, "If the black pearls are so rare, why they are available in jewelry stores most everywhere?"

Again, she looked at me in almost disbelief. She explained that the black pearls are plentiful today because they are all cultivated in oyster beds around the world --- not the natural black pearls that come only from the lagoons around Tahiti. She knew of a shop in Moorea where we could buy real black pearls directly from the divers of the families who own property around these lagoons. She would pick out each perfect pearl for the necklace she wanted to leave to Mae and have them strung right there on the site.

She added, "You do know that most black pearls are not really black? They are dark shades of green and lavender, with hints of gold and that's what makes them so beautiful. They appear black until you look more closely. Some even have a tint of rose. Black pearls are really like people. You have to look closely to see their beauty. I want to pick out the most beautiful ones for my necklace. Mae is too young now to really know about pearls. I hope she will learn these legends when she grows up --- then she will know how much I really loved her."

***

My first wife, Jenny, and I had three boys who were teenagers when she died from lung cancer. Kevin, our oldest son, was in his second year of college in Texas. Stuart, our middle son, had just graduated from high school and was going to LSU for the fall term. Andrew --- he always preferred to be called Drew --- our youngest son, decided to come back from prep school in Austin to be at home with me for his senior year in high school.

We had a nice home on the Vermilion River just south of Lafayette, Louisiana, but it was very empty with Jenny gone. She had been the center of our family for many years as I was busy with my business as President of Offshore Logistics Inc. We had started the company in 1969 with two small crew boats. Ten years later, as part of the international oil business, we had 2,500 employees and operations in twenty-five countries around the world with our combined aviation and marine activities. In Lafayette, we were a big fish in a small pond.

Everything in life is a trade off. Can you really provide what your family needs with a nine to five job ... or does it take more than that to make things really work? I don't know, but I was away from home many days and nights. I missed too many of the boys' activities to mention. Jenny was always there for them, but now she was gone.

It was a difficult time for us all.

***

Joanne came into my life by the most unusual circumstances. In the late 1970s, I had flown out to a drilling rig in the North Sea with a photographer from Aberdeen to film two of our companies' largest anchor handling supply boats move the massive rig to a new location.

The huge semi-submersible rig was owned by Global Marine and was under contract to Shell Oil Company. I had made arrangements with Shell to ride out on one of the helicopters they had under contract with Bristow Aviation, who serviced most of their North Sea operations. In an amazing turn of events, some years later, we acquired Bristow Aviation and changed the name of our company from Offshore Logistics to The Bristow Group. That story will be part of another memoir I'm working on, which will be called *The Bayou Boys*.

The weather was typical for the North Sea in winter --- with high winds and big seas --- so it would be a dramatic opportunity for us to get some great pictures to use in our annual shareholder report. After we landed on the helicopter deck, we were directed to the main dining room to meet the Drill Captain, who was in charge of the operation. He was just finishing a meeting with a group of senior rig personnel, all dressed in bright yellow survival suits and wearing yellow hard hats --- all but one. There was a very attractive, blonde young woman in all white. She wore a white survival jump suit and white hard hat, and she held a clipboard to check the personnel roster with the drill captain. I thought, *what in the hell is a woman doing out here, and a pretty one at that?*

I introduced myself, along with the photographer, to the Drill Captain and smiled at the lady in white. We shook hands all around, but they had a job to do and there was not much time for small talk. Jack, the photographer, and I had on red survival suits issued by the Bristow in Aberdeen. He nodded to me. "This would make a great picture for the cover with all these bright colors."

I replied, "Not now --- let's just get out of the way and up on deck where you can set up your cameras."

Later that day, in the helicopter on the way in from the rig, I wondered about that lady because in twenty years in the oil business I had never before seen a woman on an offshore rig.

A dozen or so passengers were riding in the Super Puma back to Aberdeen. During the hour long ride, I asked the fellow sitting next to me about her.

"Oh, that's Joanne. She's out here all the time." he replied. "Its crew-change day and she's in charge of personnel for the rig." After a pause, he said, "She'll be coming in on the last chopper tonight." After another pause, he said, "But don't get any big ideas --- she really knows her stuff."

I didn't say anything more. At the time, I was happily married when I visited that oil rig.

***

After Jenny died, it was awkward for me to begin dating in our small town --- I was just another eligible bachelor in an oil-boom town. One day in 1980, Kent, our personnel manger, came into my office with a problem. I don't remember what it was, but before he left, he invited me to a cocktail party he and Judy were having on Friday. He actually insisted that I come. He said, "At a personnel conference the other day, I met a lady who has just moved here, and I think you two would have a lot in common --- she's coming to dinner."

I looked at him, "Oh no --- no blind dates at my age."

"Just come by for a few minutes, you don't have to stay for dinner if you don't want to, but please at least come by for a drink."

Well, I did. There were a lot of my old tennis friends --- we had a very active tennis group in Lafayette. When I arrived, I saw Kent standing there with an attractive lady who looked familiar but I couldn't place her. He signaled me to come over. When we were introduced, the lady said, "How did your pictures turn out?"

The woman in the white jump suit was now in a black cocktail dress with a long strand of white pearls and diamond earrings. It was Joanne.

I stayed for dinner.

It turned out Global Marine had transferred her to the Gulf of Mexico to be personnel manager of a new and larger rig. She had proven herself in the rough-and-tumble business of the oil industry and our paths crossed again after three years. We were married about a year later.

Joanne had been married before, but did not have any children. My boys were a little hesitant when I told them I was planning to marry again. Kevin was the first to comment. "Dad, whatever makes you happy is what I want --- don't worry about me."

Stuart didn't say anything but I could tell he was not happy. It was many years later that I learned why ... and maybe that is part of the next memoir.

Drew, who was living at home at that time, was open to a new life, and seemed to be happy to have the house busy again. This was the beginning of a new love story.

Joanne didn't ask anything --- she just wanted to be

herself --- and hoped my boys would accept her. Drew was open to the idea and the two of them developed a great relationship during that first year.

In the middle of all of this was Eula Mae. She had been part of our family since Jenny and I had moved to Lafayette in 1960. She was our housekeeper, but in the tradition of the Old South, she was much more than that. Eula Mae was part of our family and helped Jenny raise the boys. Actually, she was our mother in many ways. She was always there and always in control of the situation. It was a love story that has no end.

The "Eula Mae stories" are an important part of my family. Jenny's funeral service was in the Episcopal Church of Ascension in Lafayette, where we raised our children and they went to the day school she help start. The five of us sat in the first pew: Kevin, Stuart, Andrew, Eula Mae and me.

When went forward to share Communion at the altar rail, Eula Mae stopped and touched the casket. In a voice that resonated in the packed sanctuary, she began to wail, "Oh Lordy. Oh Lordy. I have just lost my best friend."

There was not a dry eye to be found anywhere.

Drew's daughter's name is Marie. His mother's name was also Marie but everyone knew her as Jenny. When Drew, and his beautiful wife, Jean, had their first child, she was also named Marie. but we always called her Mae. Jean and Drew also decided that Mae's middle name would be Davis --- Joanne's family name. The bond within our family is very special indeed.

CHAPTER 15

REGENT SOUTH PACIFIC JOURNAL #9

Latitude '0' Longitude '0' Temperature: gorgeous
Heading: Facing downtown Papeete

Gracious good day:

This has truly been one of those milestone / memorable / magical days! We sailed from Nuku Hiva to Papeete (close to 1,000 miles) and arrived in the harbor at 8:00 AM this morning. Any semblance between these two "communities" is planets apart (almost literally and figuratively) – as Nuku Hiva is a large island but with only 2,000 inhabitants that comprises a simple, basic and happy lifestyle. Papeete, the city, and Tahiti, the island, is 100,000 +/- and the core of these South Pacific archipelagos. We are docked, as opposed to dropping the "parking hook" and are smack dab in the middle of town. In a way it's similar to a small Honolulu with traffic, businesses – yet framed by the most majestic, unspoiled green mountains imaginable ... quite an oxymoron.

    Once again we arose early because we love coming into port and experiencing the intricacies of the docking process and celebrating a new port of call. Since we have unusual shore excursions *planned for Moorea and Bora Bora, we elected to meander around Papeete on our own which was a delight. Again, French is the mother language here, however a few more people speak English and with my awkward French and their awkward English, we communicated quite well. The temperature is extraordinary ... balmy paradise with a profusion of blooming trees (plumeria being my favorite), a busy harbor with endless ferries transporting people to Moorea and Bora Bora. My only egregious disappointment was the existence of MacDonald's !! We didn't see any other western fast food eateries, but MacDonald's is like a virus – it seems to show up everywhere – I'm surprised Neil Armstrong didn't have a Big Mac on the moon!*

Despite being a booming city, it's charming – with the usual tourist shops – but a spectacular open air market (easily a city block in size) is plopped in the center of town purveying everything from the most vibrant tropical flowers to recognizable and unrecognizable vegetables and fruits, pareos (colorful hand painted fabric that is worn as garments – sort of like Indian saris), stunning jewelry made from shells (NOT tacky by any means), and an endless variety of other wares.

A spectacular evening onboard with Tahitian entertainment was planned for tonight and having just returned to our stateroom from this event, I can share that both of us are on "emotional overload." To think of the work involved to transform the pool area into a tropical wonderland (flowers, palm fronds, etc.); feeding the entire ship's complement; magnificent entertainment: the variety, presentation and quality of the "Polynesian bar-b-que" was truly over the top complete with suckling pigs AND crawfish that arrived fresh today ... HELLO!

We then relocated to the main theatre where we witnessed the most stunning Tahitians dancers: the exquisite grace of their movements .... and then those HIPS!!! It's easy to understand why the crews of the 18th century European explorers went AWOL in these islands refusing to return to their politically restrictive and *socially confining countries, having experienced the freedom, joy, hedonism and lushness in this part of the world.*

Tomorrow morn we're off for a quick relocation from Papeete to Moorea (only 11 miles) where I will find my black pearls and then later we've booked a photographic safari into the "hinterland". Moorea is easily viewed from the harbor and it's an apparition of beauty and grandeur ... we're looking forward to the adventure.

We have become more than acquaintances with Terry Waite – we are now good friends. We have had an opportunity to spend quality time with him and underscore the impact his lectures have had on those of us who have heard him ... I thanked him for sharing such personal experiences and surviving!!

Every day – every day – has been magnificent with unexpected and delightful events enhancing the adventure. We are savoring each day as it unfolds--more than words can express.

With our balcony door open as I type this, we're being entertained by Polynesian music drifting from a nightclub across the street – not intrusive – simply punctuating a remarkable day -- in paradise.

Our love, Joanne & Ken

CHAPTER

16

REGENT SOUTH PACIFIC JOURNAL #10

Longitude: 17 deg 24' 16"S Latitude: 150 deg 01' 00" W
Heading: 292 deg – Temp: 81 deg

Greetings from Paradise (...really!)
We had a quick sail from Papeete to Moorea (15 miles) this morning – and found ourselves embraced by an island that has been acknowledged through the ages as the most beautiful in the South Pacific (competing with Bora Bora).
I have no words to describe our experiences today. Normally I'm verbose with my adjectives and hyperbole but none of it could capture the extraordinary natural grandeur of this volcanic masterpiece. There are just several openings in the atoll that surrounds the island - entering either Cook or Opunohu Bays and the captain chose Cook Bay – where we dropped the "parking hook" – framed by dramatic cliffs, with clouds obscuring the tops, only to move off and present craggy spires that are reminiscent of gothic cathedrals.
We were 'tendered' into shore and our mission was to find the black pearl shop I had read about. It was a delightful experience since it is a family owned business that is major source of the real

natural black pearls. While they also farm their own oyster beds, I now proudly wear a lustrous natural black pearl necklace with matching earrings that encompasses the color range of "black" pearls. The owner's daughter, Anna, helped me pick out each of the 47 pearls for the necklace ... she was as pretty a young girl as I have ever seen. She seemed excited about my quest and we bonded right there at the shop on the lagoon.

I've worn them all day ... my entire outfit being sensible Strecker shoes; jeans; a $20 t-shirt; adorned with elegant pearls. I never asked Ken what the pearls cost because he said "it doesn't matter." Taking him at his word, I chose to have the necklace made 36 inches long with a special clasp so that they can be worn as a single loop or shorten to make for a double loop or even as a choker depending on the mood or the occasion.

While I was picking out each of the pearls in my necklace, Ken went on a walking tour of the lagoon with the owner. He asked that we join him for lunch with his family at their home overlooking the vast deep blue Pacific Ocean. While at lunch (I'm not quite sure what the fish was but it was delicious), one of their craftsmen strung the pearls into a necklace. It was just what I wanted and I'm thrilled to be wearing my necklace at this very moment.

After lunch we hurried back to the ship to join our photographic safari: only 6 people with a professional photographer, we drove around the island culminated by a harrowing drive into the interior where we ascended (by foot) a "mountain" that provided views of the island, lagoon, atoll and ocean that left out mouths hanging open as we tried to absorb the unimaginable beauty of it all: hues of blue and green that are impossible to describe.

As part of the trip, we visited one of the over-the-water 5 star hotels (Inter-Continental) that also protects dolphins and rehabilitates injured sea turtles. We saw both and congratulated the hotel for its sensitivity. The dolphins (whatever the species) are enormous and swim at an extraordinary speed ... amazing creatures. Once recovered, they're returned to the sea.

We were on the last tender to return to the ship (at sunset) – and as we left the Cook Bay, the Captain announced were going to have an impromptu sunset tour of the Opunohu Bay – an even narrower opening with the mountain, Bali, beckoning us at the head of the Bay.

Again, mere words cannot capture the colors of the sunset as the setting sun's rays played off the craggy and somewhat foreboding spires. As if that wasn't a senses' overload, the Captain played the music from "South Pacific" featuring "Bali Hi". There was a huge gathering of passengers on the top deck witnessing The Moment and we were all in awe!! The wind picked up as we left the Bay and as I couldn't keep my wig on, so I took if off with my weird hair (or lack of it) ... no one even batted an eye other than commenting on my fabulous black pearl necklace!!! Life is good!

After a full, active and exhilarating day ... we elected to have room service on the verandah as we watched Moorea fade into the distance and the constellations of the southern hemisphere began to fill the sky.

Early tomorrow, upon our arrival, we will compare the lure and beauty of Bora Bora to that of Moorea.

Sending our love and ebullience!
Joanne & Ken

CHAPTER

17

REGENT SOUTH PACIFIC JOURNAL #11 & 12

Latitude 19° 45'" 59"S Longitude 157° 21' 26"W
Heading 238° Temperature 83°

We are now between Bora Bora and Roratonga.
 I'm now becoming reluctant to state the journal number because it means the days are diminishing. I want to plug a big nail into the calendar so it never moves! Excuse the delay in the journals 11 & 12, but the internet connection is capricious out here in the vast Pacific. So, here's our day in Bora Bora and at sea today:
 No doubt you've all seen photos of this fantasy island Bora Bora, sheltered in the middle of a huge lagoon and guarded by a coral atoll! The endless hues of blue as the water depth changes; and the endless hues of tropical greenery – again make adjectives superfluous. There is only one natural break in the coral atoll allowing entrance into the lagoon, then the "parking hook" was dropped and we tendered into town.
 We are continually learning about the extraordinary history of these islands (dating B.C.) – but more contemporary information is that the USN SeaBees were stationed in Bora Bora during WWII, building bunkers, docks, gun emplacements, runway (which

is used today), roads and other infracture. As there is only one access to the island, guarding it wasn't too difficult and what an assignment!!! Love to know how many of today's inhabitants are descendants of their "visit" here.

So, we experienced the efforts of the Seabees by traveling completely around the island on a road built by them on Le Truk – which is a bastardized-type school bus, brightly painted and with fresh flowers decorating both the inside and out. What a touch as it mitigated the rather inadequate shock absorbers as we bounced along, visually staggered by the incredibly natural scenic beauty greeting us at every turn in the road. Tropical flowers that we consider so exotic and rare in a local arrangement, grow in profusion, i.e., ginger, birds of paradise, plumeria, hibiscus, etc. most used as hedges. The latest movie version of "Mutiny on the Bounty" with Mel Gibson and Anthony Hopkins was filmed on Bora Bora, whereas the 1980's film was done on Moorea. Our guide was quick to point out Marlon Brando's home where he resided with Tarita during that filming (can hardly wait to use that info at our next cocktail party!)

The ultimate romantic fanciful hotels all are bungalows built on stilts over the water of the lagoon. Ken and I had planned to lunch at the new Four Seasons – but learned that evidently cruise passengers are "undesirables" and are charged $75 per person for the privilege of spending more money for a meal!!! We fully understand that guests paying $1,500 per night per person (meals extra) do not need an invasion of "outsiders" ... but it still seemed a bit over-the-top.

Instead, we lunched at another famous landmark – Bloody Marys – a great character in "South Pacific", now a highly successful "watering hole". The elaborate entrance has a painted board identifying all the famous people who have sipped a Bloody Mary at "Bloody Mary's", LaDamanian Tomlinson, Sen. McCain, Nicole Kidman, Pierce Brosnan – and I would certainly hope to see OUR names there one day!!

Now having the opportunity to visit/explore both Moorea and Bora Bora – Moorea is minimally populated and geologically much more dramatic than Bora Bora. "BB" is about 16,000 inhabitants, geologically "softer" than Moorea, but it's location in the midst of the dazzling lagoon gives it another kind of magic! Honestly, everything in the southern Pacific has an ambience and pace unknown and underappreciated by the rest of the world. The French and local Polynesian officials are cognizant of the importance of tourism, but they are protecting these islands zealously – great! As I've reported in previous journals, not only have the assortment of ports-of-call been intriguing, but the people we've met are equally intriguing and delightful.

As we departed watching Bora Bora from our stateroom disappear into the horizon, the sea began to pick up and we're delighted to be experiencing a bit of "rock and roll." Nothing to spill a wine glass nor preclude a luscious meal ... just to remind us we're at sea!

Through an interesting circumstance, Ken and I are developing a growing friendship with Terry Waite. Not only surviving his ordeal of 20 some years ago, he's now "surviving" a new ordeal I can relate to and we talk about it ... lung cancer ... and our conversations are provocative, healing and uplifting. These serendipitous meetings and connections are remarkable, indeed.

On the subject of "serendipitous meetings" ... tonight we're having dinner with a couple who BOTH attended the same high school as Ken in OKC; attended OU; same fraternity (Kappa Sigma) and were both president of said chapter (not at the same time)!!! The wife also flew for American last century. We'll have oodles to talk about!!

Tomorrow morn we anchor in Roratonga (love to say that) and we have a glass-bottom boat tour scheduled in/on their lagoon; lunch on an uninhabited island (sort of a Robinson Crusoe touch). Then we'll mosey around town ... again rife with 18th and 19th century history - revolving around the European explorers, followed *by the lousy missionaries (I think you get my drift that I'm not enamored with their influence on these exquisite Polynesian people and their culture that existed for thousands of years).*

It's now 1830 hrs somewhere in the Pacific and we're dressing for our Oklahoma din/din.

Sending our love, Joanne & Ken

CHAPTER 18

JANUARY 25, 2009

We had dinner with our new friends from Oklahoma. Later, as we left Bora Bora in "our rear view mirror," daylight slowly drifted away and the moon came up over the horizon after another magnificent day in paradise. What more can anyone say? It is truly one of the great opportunities to enjoy God's miracles.

As Joanne wrote her journal that night, I stayed on the veranda and watched the darkening sky looking for the Southern Cross. Even though I had been on boats and ships all over the world, I had not given much thought until that night that the constellations in the Northern Hemisphere were different from those south of the equator.

One of the great pleasures in my life was sailing from Maine to the Caribbean each fall, either on CRACKERS, my thirty-six foot sailboat, or helping others make the 1,500 mile trip. The skies at night became a familiar road map, and I would just steer the boat by the stars for hours at a time. The North Star, the Big Dipper, Orion's Belt and many others were there to guide me on my way. I never tired of the midnight watch --- just me and the silence of a small boat making its way in the vast open ocean restores your soul in ways that are hard to explain.

The skies in the Southern Hemisphere were new to me. I looked for the familiar landmarks but to no avail. There was so much to learn and every trip on the oceans of the world is a new adventure.

From time to time I would look back into the stateroom to watch Joanne typing away on her journal. It was becoming more obvious each day that Dr. Radford's prediction was coming true. In the past few days, Joanne was showing more symptoms of carcinomatous meningitis --- the spread of the cancer cells to the tissues surrounding the brain. In addition to her balance, I felt that she was also beginning to have an issue with her hearing and vision. She never complained about it but I could see the little changes each day.

Joanne finished her typing and came out to join me on the veranda. She commented that she was becoming more forgetful and couldn't remember names as well as she had in the past. Trying to be more positive I said, "You have an unbelievable recall for names --- maybe you are just getting older and you are becoming more like the rest of us."

She replied, "No, no, that's not the problem. In writing my journal tonight, I wanted to mention the name of that nice couple from Oklahoma we just had dinner with, but their names escaped me. I have always had a good recall of names ever since flying for Pan Am. We were trained to remember the names of our passengers and who was in each seat --- Mr. Smith from Chicago was in 2B, Mrs. Brown from San Francisco was in 3C --- things like that. We spoke to them by their name; it was just part of the training. It just showed that you were interested in them and the habit has stuck with me all these years since."

I smiled and said, "I can't remember their names either, so don't worry about that."

She reached over and took my hand. "I know my days are numbered, and the things that Dr. Radford said would happen are beginning to add up. I only ask two things of you; one, please remember me for all the good times we have had together; and two, I don't want you to sit at home all by yourself when I'm gone." Then she added, "I want you to find a new companion."

I interrupted, "Now don't get too far ahead of yourself. Who knows what will happen next. Wives usually live longer than their husbands --- and besides that, you were my child bride."

But she wouldn't let it go. "I mean it. I want you to find someone who is tall and blonde --- someone like Karen --- who will drive you a little crazy the way I have, but who can also play golf."

After a minute or two of silence, I said, "You are really a match maker. But if the roles are reversed, then I want you to have a companion who is rich and loves to travel --- and can dance like Fred Astaire."

CHAPTER 19

REGENT SOUTH PACIFIC JOURNAL #13

Latitude 22° 26' 17" S Longitude 161° 55' 16" W
Heading 238° Temp 79° Speed 18 knots

Hi out there!

I'm most distressed to tell you that there's been a glitch in paradise – Roratonga sank!

Actually, the island is notorious for wicked sea swells as well as unruly currents and today we were bombarded with both. Our "eye candy/central casting" captain tried, in vain, numerous times to set the anchor as there isn't a harbor, per se. Then the use of the tenders was attempted, but with waves breaking over the boarding platform and the tender heaving 6 ft up and down – it was prudently decided to bypass Roratonga.

As there are a number of quite 'senior citizens' onboard, the image of these people being heaved into the tender (or missing it altogether) conjures up an unpleasant image. It would have been "swell" to visit Roratonga but the swells prohibited another island adventure. However, having experienced the splendor of Tahiti, Moorea and Bora Bora, missing Roratonga isn't as grim as it could have been if this was our only South Pacific island. However,

I feel sorry for me having arisen at 6:00 AM to join an excursion ... but more importantly I feel sorry for the Roratongans as our visit would have been a boost to their local economy.

We now have an extra day at sea .... so my subsequent reports will be sea conditions and onboard activities. However, with the "free time" I actually put on a swimming costume and sat in the sun for a brief time. Neither of us can remember the last time I did this, but it felt delicious and I'm gradually gaining a bit of the "Bronze Goddess" look. Ahhhh, the simple pleasures of life!

It was remarkable how the cruise personnel adjusted to the change in schedule and had a new one prepared and printed in about 45 minutes. The various lecturers rose to the occasion so we've attended and have learned: "The demise of the Germans in the South Pacific" (we didn't know they ever had encampments in this area); "Everything you wanted to know about Burma, but were afraid to ask"; an hour with Terry Waite devoted to Q&A only; and information and suggestions of what to do when we visit Picton, located on the most northeastern corner of NZ's south island (where we'll dock). At our next Kenmure gathering we'll either be scintillating or downright bores with all this acquired information!

Picton and the surrounding region is an important wine area and one of our favorites, Cloudy Bay, is grown there. Needless to say, we're taking that excursion which also includes a gourmet lunch – count us in!!!! We'll then "gunk hole" down the eastern coast of NZ with stops at Auckland, Christchurch, Timaru, Akaroa – then 'round the southern tip to meander through Dusky, Doubtful and Milford Sounds .... we ask for a gorgeous day for the trip through these fjords.

It's dinner time and after an exhausting day of basically doing nothing we're famished.

More on the ocean tomorrow ....
Our love, Joanne & Ken

CHAPTER 20

REGENT SOUTH PACIFIC JOURNALS #14 & 15

Latitude 31°00' 07"S Longitude 177° 05' 40"W
Heading 240° Temp 72°

We have no idea where we are as early this morning we crossed the International Date Line, losing Wednesday, but still en route from our aborted visit at Roratonga to New Zealand and the Bay of Islands -- distance of 1,000+ miles!

For those of you who have been to the UK and listened to the rather vague and offhanded weather reports, then you'll appreciate my report from "at sea": it has been fine, less than fine, some sun, no sun and back to relatively fine!! The sea and wind did pick up a bit and it was delicious negotiating the rolling of the ship and particularly at night when we were 'rocked' to sleep.

Ken has timed my exposure to the sun (sort of like turning on a rotisserie) and I actually having bathing suit strap marks which I consider a triumph ... my memory doesn't reach that far back as to last time I enjoyed a "tan".

Many of you have asked about Terry Waite and his profound and important messages regarding his captivity and literally how he survived. Being in solitary confinement for actually 4 years, he relied on his "center core" meaning who he was and concentrating on his personal strengths and mitigating weaknesses that were destructive. He "wrote a book" in his mind, that has subsequently been published ("Taken in Trust") and while in Auckland we will try and find it. The audience asked many provocative questions about his "revenge", recovery, etc etc. He does not harbor any animosity towards his captors because it is a useless emotion and only the person holding the rage is hurt by it.

When asked about his emotional and physical recovery upon returning home, he said that his entire family spent time with a counselor that was healing and important. He praises his wife for raising their 4 children during his absence and to the Anglican Church (he worked for the Archbishop) for providing financial support to his family during this trauma. He's a truly extraordinary person; open and willing to share any information; and with a raucous sense of humor. He has endeared himself to everyone!!

I had one more chat with him this afternoon regarding his visit to the Kanuga Conference Center (amazing) and to share our current health issues. He has shared deep, comforting and uplifting thoughts and philosophies with me. Once again, I feel blessed with how each day unfolds …. and certainly here, somewhere in the middle of the Pacific.

Everything is "fine" …
Our love, Joanne & Ken

CHAPTER 21

REGENT SOUTH PACIFIC JOURNAL #16

Latitude 36° 50' 30"S Longitude 174° 4' 06"E
Temp 68° Humidity 96%

LAND HO!!
  We have traveled over 6,000 miles literally in the lap of luxury – this was NOT the style of Capt. Cook and his intrepid crew by any means – but we have visited many of his initial ports of call and if something doesn't have a Maori or Polynesian name, it's "Cook"!
  We eased into Bay of Islands (not "the" ... simply Bay of Islands) yesterday - and it is, yet another area where adjectives are superfluous! Good 'ol Capt. Cook counted 144, but probably more accurately is +/- 100 ... each more stunning than the next with dramatically changing topography. One island is tropical, the next looks like the dramatic cliffs of Scotland; then luscious green like Ireland; with arid islands akin to Bakersfield, CA!!! The water is absolutely pristine …. and…. we had one of those spectacularly magnificent days: fluffy clouds, azure blue skies – and the tropical waters!
  As it is summer time south of the equator, and we were there on a Saturday, the bay was full of boats of every description and size.

I was particularly intrigued with a tour boat called the "Exciter" that has the look of a cigarette boat, with speed to match, throwing off a huge rooster tail in its wake. We opted for a more sedate vessel that didn't create any sort of whiplash when the engine was started!!

Our tour of the islands, observing the beauty, included several privately owned islands with "holiday homes" that were enormous. One island is owned by an American (no names, no bank name) but his house is an architectural wonder: long and narrow, with 11 levels providing a view that leaves one agape. Ahhh, the joys of capitalism (whatever is left of it!)

The highlight of the trip was actually passing through an eroded hole in one of the islands (with an all-women crew, I might add) and the master-ette of the vessel had the "touch" as there was only about 25 ft on either side of the boat. I loved it!!

We were then deposited at the enchanting town of Russell – when we lunched at the oldest licensed hotel in NZ: The Lord Marlborough Inn, right on the water. I had green lipped mussels (beyond succulent) and Ken reveled in the best fish 'n chips ever. Now fortified, we roamed around the town, replete with charming Victorian architecture, flowers everywhere – children playing in the water ... just magical.

We then 'tendered' back to the boat, however, we had company in the form of "Rhapsody of the Seas" – one of the 2,500 passenger Royal Caribbean behemoths. We had hoped to nab position 'A' at the dock in Auckland, but our ship suffered an interesting glitch upon both the ships' departures from the Bay – the magnetic compass "died". The eye candy/central casting captain advised we'd have to travel around in circles to "swing" the compass in order to correct the problem. I'm pleased to advise that the "G" forces of this process in no way catapulted us to the side of the ship, much less disturbed our wine glasses nor our ability to put fork to mouth.

Once fixed and heading in the right direction, we were given a joyful treat in that hundreds of leaping dolphins escorted us out into the ocean causing great excitement on board. However, ye 'ol Rhapsody had left us in her dust/wake and when we arrived in Auckland this morning, there she was in Position 'A'. Drat!!

From our stern stateroom, we have watched as the America's Cup-style sailboats are being towed to the racing venue. This is called the Louis Vuitton Pacific Regatta. We can see the course from our balcony and with binoculars witness the flying spinnakers, etc. Good stuff!

Many passengers disembarked in Auckland; including our new friend Terry Waite ... it is a glorious feeling to be "in transit".

More later,
G'Day, Joanne & Ken

CHAPTER 22

REGENT SOUTH PACIFIC JOURNAL #17

Auckland, NZ

Hi Everyone!
 I haven't included the nautical information, because we're now ashore in Auckland taking a brief hiatus – then rejoining the ship in Christchurch on Wednesday the 4th.
 We're staying at a new Hilton literally hanging over the water with a "harbor" view. This is a gross misnomer as our windows do face the harbor; <u>however</u>, they are darkened by enormous cruise ships that "park" about 20 ft away from us. We now have the Sun Princess as our neighbor and this morning we were entertained by a naked man doing his exercises on his balcony. Trust me, this was not a pretty sight!! I should have gone out on our balcony, naked, and done the hootchy-kootchy. He would have either fallen overboard or suffered some cardio infarction!!
 However, on the other side of the hotel is the America's Cup or Louis Vuitton Pacific Regatta Village!!! Ken can barely contain his joy as not only are the racing boats moored there, but the most astounding collection of mega-yachts. Evidently, these people did

not get the memo about global recession…. Of course, I'm taking zillions of photos.

Auckland, a city of 1.3 million, behaves like a "village": clean, organized, extremely friendly, greenery everywhere … and with its motto of "City of Sails" – the harbor is simply covered with rowboats, ferries, sexy sailboats of every size, and motor yachts …. How much "eye candy" can a person absorb?!?

As a note, we just watched the Super Bowl (live). Obviously it evolved into a great game. It began at noon NZ time on Monday 2 Feb. Now we're watching (live) the sailboat races as they occur just outside the harbor. Good stuff!

Tomorrow we're spending all day at the Louis Vuitton Village, then our flight to Christchurch departs mid-day on Wednesday and we'll board the 'mother ship' about 6 PM. The itinerary continues to Timaru, the Dusky, Doubtful & Milford Sounds, Tasmania – then Sydney. During that time I will have chained myself to something immovable 'cuz it's tough to consider leaving perfection!

Happy days, from Auckland
Joanne & Ken

CHAPTER 23

REGENT SOUTH PACIFIC JOURNAL #18

Auckland, NZ

Think of the song lyrics: "...what a day this has been, what a rare mood I'm in ...." and that will serve as a preamble to this day in Auckland... stunning!

As planned, we visited the Louis Vuitton Pacific Regatta Village (which is literally next to our hotel) and our timing was perfect as the racing boats were all departing their berths for the contests at hand.

For our landlubber pals the following information won't mean much, but for our fellow sailors and particularly those who live in Maine ... THE <u>Endeavor</u> is moored among the "big boys". She is as elegant and well maintained as she was while she graced Penobscot Bay. It was nostalgic to see her!!

As previously discussed, the "spectator yachts" dazzle the senses – sailboats and motorboats that are 150' to 250' in length; crews scurrying around their respective vessels in matching outfits attending to the myriad of details that keep them gleaming and with nary a fingerprint!! Simply a treat to be an observer.

And the weather today …..idyllic… and we squeezed lots of

experiences out of such a magnificent day: meandering around the city – then taking a ferry to Devenport which is an enchanting Victorian section of Auckland that overlooks the harbor (seems everything overlooks the harbor). Again, for a city this size there is NO graffiti anywhere; there is a civility and national pride that seems to have been lost in other parts of our globe; and, yes, we're completely enamored with New Zealand.

Tomorrow we fly to Christchurch where we'll rejoin the 'mother ship' for our continuing itinerary to Timaru, the Sounds (Dusky, Doubtful and Milford), Tasmania – then Sydney and a side visit to the Blue Mountains.

My glowing reports about this trip may have become a bit redundant ... but I'm only giving you the facts, ma'am ... in every respect it has far exceeded our wildest expectations.

Next report will be from the ship after visiting Christchurch and en route to Timaru.

Sending our love,
Joanne & Ken

CHAPTER 24

FEBRUARY 4, 2009

During the days after Moorea, where she found her very own black pearl necklace, she began to have a serious problem swallowing. We would always dress for dinner where she could eat and enjoy the taste; however, the food just stuck in her throat. She would excuse herself from the table, only to return a few minutes later to rejoin in the conversation as if nothing had happened.

We reviewed Dr. Radford's protocol. This was one of the many signs the cancer cells had spread to the brain which could no longer coordinate the normal process of eating. It was a surprise at first but then it began to make sense. Joanne could enjoy the taste but not the nourishment that came from eating and she was slowly losing weight.

But what to do now? We contacted Leann through email and she quickly came back with an appointment with a doctor we should see in Auckland --- an old friend of Dr. Radford's who would have her medical history when we arrived. Just saying we were getting off for a day or two to visits friends, we packed an overnight case and left the ship in Auckland for a visit with Dr. Pulkingham.

In its own way, this was amazing. He turned his practice over to see what he could do for Joanne. Within the next twenty-four hours, he did a CT scan, an MRI, and a complete blood work-up.

He then shared his thoughts. He concurred with Dr. Radford that Joanne's situation was only a matter of time. Her systems were shutting down. She would probably find her sight and her balance becoming bigger problems each day.

In the discussions with Dr. Pulkingham, Joanne explained, that in addition to finding her black pearls, how important it was that we continue on to see Milford Sound --- one of her main objectives in planning this cruise. We had been to New Zealand several times in years past but on each visit the weather was too bad to enter the sounds at the southern tip of the South Island. This would be her last chance.

He agreed that there was nothing to gain by giving up now --- and he felt she could probably make it another week to Sydney before we had to "abandon ship."

So when Joanne wrote in her Journal, that we had taken a little hiatus in Auckland to visit friends, she never mentioned the real reason we had left the ship for a few days. No one reading her journals would ever have known. And no one on the ship would ever know what had really happened --- but it was only the beginning.

We decided to rejoin the ship at the next available port. When checking out of the Hilton, however, we could not find her black pearl necklace. We looked in and around the room safe, under the bed, and; we even moved the furniture. We looked everywhere but there was no black pearl necklace.

What could have happened? Even though she had worn them everyday since finding her pearls in Moorea, she remembered that she could not wear any jewelry during the MRI yesterday. She thought she had possibly left them on the room safe rather than putting them away. When we finally realized they were actually gone, she was devastated. After a few moments, she had a complete emotional breakdown. It was the most heart wrenching experience I have ever known. I held her close as she began to cry. Shaking almost uncontrollably, she said, "I'm losing my eye sight --- I'm losing my life --- I'm losing you --- and now, I've lost my black pearl necklace."

We sat and cried together. After almost an hour, she looked up, wiped the tears from her eyes, and said, "Well, we have a plane to catch so we don't want to be late."

I reported the loss to the hotel and we went on to the airport for the flight to Christchurch and the drive on to the port of Lyttelton. Her "hiatus" she had referred to was a devastating experience, however, you would never know it from the upbeat reports in her journals.

CHAPTER 25

REGENT SOUTH PACIFIC JOURNAL #19

Latitude 43° 51' 06" S Longitude 173° 12' 51" E
Heading 202° Temp 60°

Greetings:

It is wonderful to be back on the ship and offshore again. Our relocation from Auckland to Christchurch, however, was both enterprising and amusing! The flight arrived in Christchurch around 4:00 PM – then about a 30 mile drive to Lyttelton. Our rather flamboyant Russian taxi driver announced that the Regent was expected to arrive at 5:00 PM which was ideal. However, further inquiry pushed it back to 6:30 PM. Now we had our luggage and time to kill with no place to wait! I had no intention of sitting on my luggage at an industrial dock – which we couldn't have done anyway because we weren't "authorized".

As a digression, Lyttelton is a seaman's town dating back to the late 18th century and a great number of the original buildings relating to the sailing trade still exist. They all seemed to have evolved into rather seedy quay-side bars and questionable *hostelries – certainly not where we would have wished to bide our time waiting for our ship to come in!!*

So, we asked our flamboyant Russian taxi driver to cruise around town in an attempt to find a reasonable place to light – which we did in the form of The Irish Pub which had windows overlooking the harbor. Before schlepping in our bags, Ken told the bartender our situation wherein he enthusiastically proclaimed: "Come on in, mates."

The New Zealanders are fabulously open and friendly people and soon we were invited to join a birthday party; everyone in the bar was captivated by our story of having sailed from Los Angeles – from the western mountains of NC – dragging around luggage – and joining a cruise ship in their town. We were treated a bit like friendly aliens. The women were crazy about my "hair" and long fingernails – what a hoot! Then we all saw the bow of the 'mother ship' round the point and ease into the harbor and it was a joy to see her. The ship presented the picture of a gorgeous woman entering a room full of derelicts because Lyttelton is a working harbor with coal and lumber being loaded on rusty ships; smelly old fishing boats, etc.--- not pristine in their appearance. The Regent looked like Cinderella-at-the-ball.

We asked for a taxi wherein the bartender said "nay, mates – I'll have one of my friends in Port Security come and pick you up." An official van showed up at the bar and a rather taciturn "security" person scowled at us and the luggage – but managed to thaw a bit by the time we reached the ship. I looked upon his demeanor as a challenge and used my feminine wiles to urge a smile. Bingo!

We were graciously welcomed back onboard into the bosom of comfort and pampering, and entering our stateroom to see our stuff that we hadn't packed for our stay in Auckland, was akin to being home again.

While we were in Auckland, we bought a book on the southern constellations (which are totally different that those north of the

Equator) and as I write this, Ken is on the verandah verifying the stars and how they relate to the constellations – he's a happy man!!

Today, rather than venturing back into Christchurch (where we've been before) we explored Lyttelton as there is great maritime history. We're not exactly museum people but there is a particularly poignant one dedicated to the intrepid explorers of the Antarctic, including Scott and Shackelton. As a note, Christchurch is the launching area for expeditions to the Antarctic.

Another fascinating relic of the past exists here and that is a Time Ball Station .... What is that you ask (please tell me you're asking?!) Knowing the time is critical in ocean navigation and once a reliable chronometer was invented and Greenwich Mean Time was established, it was imperative that the navigators of these 18th and 19th century ships had the correct time for longitude. All over the world, Time Ball Stations were built – high towers with a ball that descended at exactly 1:00 PM GMT. The ships in port would watch for the ball to drop then recalibrate their chronometers to ensure accurate navigation. Maybe this is a bit dull, but, coincidentally, as we arrived at the station a Japanese TV crew was filming a documentary about the harbor and station – we were shoved in front of the cameras so now we'll be on Japanese TV!! Climbing the stairs to the top was much like ascending those stone spiral stairs in old castles. WOW, we've done some walking and our legs our pooped – but terrific photos from atop the tower!!

We're now heading to Timaru for a brief shop – then en route to the much anticipated Dusky, Doubtful and Milford Sounds. Please keep your fingers crossed for luscious weather.

The temperature dropped dramatically: from the 80's in Auckland to the low 60's and a lusty wind in Lyttelton. A special friend crocheted a cozy scarf for me to take on this trip and it, gratefully, warmed my neck today.

More from Timaru et al.
Our love, Joanne & Ken

CHAPTER

26

REGENT SOUTH PACIFIC JOURNAL #20

° Latitude: 44° 49' 04" S Longitude: 167° 16' 28" E
Heading 43° - Temp 59°

Timaru and cruising the Sounds: Dusky, Doubtful & Milford
I'm disturbed that this is Journal #20 because it means this glorious odyssey is reaching a decision point and may becoming to an end – however, we do have another week and so many glorious memories. Think of the lyrics, "...they can't take that away from me..."

Before detailing our passages through arguably the most stunning spots on the globe: Fjordlands, NZ – I'll give a brief report on Timaru. Brief because our stay was just that – 8:00 AM 'til 2:00 PM; but our presence created great excitement as not only was it Regent's maiden visit to the port, but we were the first cruise ship in well over a year!!! Additionally, it was a national holiday: Waitangi Day – celebrating the treaty between the Maori's and the British in the late 1800's – where they agreed to be nice to each other.

National holidays generally translate to "no shopping" much less public attractions being open. However, Timaru is an important port and the town, itself, was charming: planters everywhere overflowing with summer flowers; hanging baskets with a profusion of posies – even the street dividers were ablaze with marigolds, etc. Most of the town's architecture dates back to the late 19th and early 20th centuries. A new rose garden (1,100 varieties) had just been dedicated several years ago.... So what does one do – stop and smell the roses. As I mentioned – there wasn't a great deal to do in Timaru. Probably the highlight was when we returned to the ship, a brass band comprised of local school children bedecked in black and yellow "outfits" serenaded us. Some of the instruments were bigger than the children, but, by gosh, they had the lung power to belt out some great toe tapping sounds!!

Much to our surprise and delight, our departure created quite a sensation (remember, first cruise ship in over a year) and the holiday, Waitangi Day, the dock and jetties were packed with people all waving and cheering us good-bye. I had wished we were in the days when passengers threw confetti from the ship ... it was all quite special.

We then headed south passing by Dunedin and through the Formeaux Strait (between the mainland and Stuart Island) for the turn north to the Sounds. Last night was formal attire – enhanced with another magnificent dinner; then a superb show with Australia's ballroom dancing champions – as well as an excellent performance by the ship's onboard singers and dancers!

This morning we were on deck early to experience entry into the first sound (a misnomer as they're really fjords, carved out by glaciers during the last Ice Age! With the endless development we continue to witness around the world, it is heartening to observe pristine and magical scenery that is untouched by the human hand. It's exactly the same as when the initial explorers discovered the area in the mid-1700's. It rains over 300" per year so the flora is abundant and so is the wildlife: porpoises, dolphins, seals and birds. The weather is unusual – with wisps of clouds hiding the peaks, then moving off to reveal jagged mountains with gushing waterfalls. It all appears mystical and like a scene from a brooding Wagnerian opera.

The drama of visiting these fjords was beautifully orchestrated by Regent as Dusky and Doubtful Sounds as mentioned above are magnificent ...... however, Milford is almost impossible to mentally process in its scope, grandeur and beauty. For those of you who have experienced Milford Sound you will understand my meager attempt to describe it – for those who haven't (like us) – it has left an indelible impression for a variety of reasons.

As we began the turn into the Sound we were a bit discouraged because the cloud level was low, obscuring the tops of the sheer cliffs. But, as the ship entered the Sound the sun was fighting to break through and it won .... clearing the vista like the opening of a stage curtain. What we witnessed was a true gift .... stunningly sheer granite and tree covered 5,000 ft mountains that disappear into the water. They are jagged, ominous and imposing – yet "softened" by breathtaking waterfalls that drop from the tops of these cliffs. Since the water is so deep the ship eased into the base of one of these waterfalls – practically touching the granite!

Another extraordinary memory maker was that in the middle of nowhere (these fjords/sounds are only accessible by water) we came across 3 kayaks. The eye candy/central casting captain stopped the ship and via loudspeaker asked the kayakers to come along side wherein he lowered them a bottle of champagne. Everyone applauded – it was so damn classy!!!

As we departed Milford, the weather and clouds closed in behind us obliterating the opening and the magnificence shrouded behind.

Now we're beginning our crossing of the Tasman Sea to Hobart, Tasmania. The "eye candy/central casting" captain has already advised that it could be rough as it's in an area called "the roaring 40's". This means open ocean with nothing to buffer the winds and sea from either Antarctica or the north. The last time we *crossed the Tasman Sea on a Silversea's cruise several years ago we "enjoyed" a Force 10 storm which certainly got our attention.*

It has been a remarkable day – Ken and I greatly anticipated visiting this part of New Zealand and as seemingly everything regarding this trip, it far exceeded our expectations.

Our love, Joanne & Ken

CHAPTER 27

REGENT SOUTH PACIFIC JOURNAL #21

Latitude 43° 15' 56" S Longitude 152° 01' 40" E
Heading 309°   Temp 56°
Crossing the Tasman Sea (the roaring 40's)

Hi Everyone!
If this writing seems a bit scribbly, it's because we're being tossed around like so much driftwood! Since departing the Milford Sound, the weather has been hellacious crossing the infamous Tasman Sea: 65+ knot winds, huge seas that bounce this big ship around as if it were a rubber ducky! However, fortunately Ken and moi never suffer any mal de mer so we nestle ourselves up to the dining table and drink our wine with nary a thought!
The heavy seas have also delayed our arrival into Hobart – so instead of 6:30 PM tonight Tasmanian time, it will be tomorrow morning. It's fabulous to contemplate what goes on behind the scenes with the administrative people, having to reorganize schedules, excursions, etc – and they all appear very unflappable.
As we rock n' roll …. more tomorrow from Tasmania.

Our love, Joanne & Ken

CHAPTER
28
REGENT SOUTH PACIFIC JOURNAL #22

Latitude 39° 28' 11" S Longitude 149° 37' 06" E
Heading 14° Temperature 60°

Hi Everyone:
  Even though my journal numbers don't total our days onboard – I've given you a detailed report of our impressions and experiences. We're stunned to realize that this month has seemingly evaporated and we will wave ta-ta to Regent on the 13th. As I have elaborated many times, this holiday has been completely flawless in every respect.
  After a truly bumpy ride across the Tasman, we eased into the sheltered and lovely harbor surrounding Hobart. Here we are in the virtual lap of luxury maybe having a bit of champagne slosh in the heavy seas – causing me to ponder the 17th and 18th century explorers, chewing on hardtack – having been at sea for eons – and discovering this welcoming harbor!
  As a quick bit of history: Tasmania began as a penal colony for the British – accepting the spillover of convicts sent to Australia. It's very much a combination of Les Miserables, Devil's Island, etc. Some of the convicts were hardened criminals; some had merely

stolen a loaf of bread – and now they were zillions of miles from Great Britain, never to see their homeland again, and spending their lives in appalling conditions relegated to hard labor!!

The convicts' legacy are gorgeous limestone buildings that are close to 200 years old and much of Hobart's architecture. The styles range from Georgian to Greek Revival and the limestone is the color of caramel sauce. Streets are lined with trees; parks full of flowers abound; people are friendly and happy to welcome tourists – and it was a beautiful day.

In the morning, Ken and I did our "walk-about", meandering up and down streets and strolling the marina that had just hosted a wooden boat regatta. Unfortunately, it had ended the day before we arrived .... Drat!

In the afternoon we took a tour of Richmond – which is a perfectly preserved "convict-built-limestone" village, wherein one could visit one of the hellish gaols (down-under for "jail") and it was eerie (if only the walls could talk).

Then off to one of the many flourishing Tasmanian wineries – this was Coal Vineyard. with only 13 acres, they distribute their product locally, but do have a contract with Canada ... of all places! The scenery was positively luscious overlooking the thriving vineyards off to the mountains and bodies of water. Very special!

Our final stop was 'Runnymeade' – a grand home built in the early 1800's by the first lawyer of Tasmania. Aaaaaaah, those lawyers and their $$$$$. It's a national trust property and presented as a home, not a museum. Think The Biltmore on a much smaller scale, but equally as impressive.

The furniture was original to the house as were the gardens – all the plants and flowers are what grew in the 1800's – very charming and informative and the guide associated with the national trust (probably in his late 70's) was akin to having George Burns show us around. We all wanted to pack him up and take him home with us ... he brought everything alive and was delightful.

Our crossing to Sydney, across the Bass Strait, still has a bit *of motion to it, but relaxing rather than an upheaval. We have a day on the ship in Sydney where we'll attend the opera and the Sydney Opera House ... then head west to the Blue Mountains for several days.*

It all seems surreal that our journey is all but complete and we would NOT have missed this opportunity for anything ... truly!

We'll send one more from Sydney tomorrow – as we don't know what will happen after that.

Happy Wednesday, to one and all...
G'Day, Joanne & Ken

CHAPTER 29

REGENT SOUTH PACIFIC JOURNAL #23

Even though we're lashed to the dock in Sydney Harbor our coordinates are:
Latitude 33° 51' 37" S Longitude 151° 12' 37"

Our friends:
It is honestly with deep sadness that we bid farewell to this magnificent ship and the extraordinary adventure it represents – on many levels!
Our entry into Sydney Harbor was just as awesome (overused word – but worthy in this instance) as myriads of photos have shown. It was one of those milestone days where I actually witnessed a <u>sunrise</u> (5:30 AM) so as not to miss one of those make-a-memory events. With the Harbour Bridge serving as a Lorelei, we rounded a bend and there was the iconic Sydney Opera House ….. and we're docked smack-dab between them – it's our view from our stern stateroom!!! Special stuff!!
Rather than take a scheduled tour, we simply put on our comfy shoes and hit the streets – which was a delight. Sydney and its environs is 4.2 million people and it is a "bouillabaisse" of architectural style from the grand Belle Époque of the 1800's

to contemporary skyscrapers that actually seem to compliment one another. All this glass and stone is softened by endless parks, sidewalk trees, and sculptures. Our favorite was the "QVB" (Queen Victoria Building) built circa 1840 and totally renovated in 1998. It is a gem – a conglomeration of all that the Victorian era produced by way of technology, "ginger-bready details", enormous glass clerestory, and enticing shops etc.

And our stop in Sydney couldn't have been culminated in a more fitting "swan song" that attending an opera at the Sydney Opera House!!! We had to pinch ourselves as a reminder we were actually inside the building and experiencing this! The two operas (generally performed together because they're relatively short) were "Cavalleria Rusticana" and "Pagliacci" – which were performed superbly. Though it's a bit difficult to become enamored with the much beloved Australian tenor as he is NOT "eye candy" – looking more like a sumo wrestler – playing this romantic role …. But his Pavrotti voice more than made up for his chubbiness.

It was raining quite hard when we left the opera building and due to the ubiquitous security we had to walk probably ½ mile to our bus. Many of the woman had had their hair done and were wearing yummy evening shoes – and they weren't too happy with the situation. Me, I'm "drip dry"!!

Ken and I have now visited three (3) major South Pacific ports: Auckland, Hobart and now Sydney. Those of you who have visited these cities know from whence I speak. The water is clean; ports are active with an endless variety of ferries; there are parks; marinas; NO graffiti – there is a national pride not very evident in ye 'ol USA. Viewing the world from the deck of a cruise ship is a beautiful and cloistered space. We haven't read a paper; listened to the news: but simply relished being embraced by unspoiled, simple and happy parts of the world. We think we're the better for it!!

We leave today for a few days in the Blue Mountains (2 hrs drive northwest of Sydney) and if we're not able to snatch the 'net' this is most likely my final journal.

There is a song with lyrics that is my mantra: "If you have the chance to sit it out or dance, I hope you dance." My dear friends – we have DANCED!!

Our love, Joanne & Ken
P.S. Heartfelt thanks for your feedback on the journal entries. It inspired me for the next one!!

CHAPTER 30

FEBRUARY 14, 2009

We left the ship knowing that Joanne could not continue on. However, let me explain --- and add a few more comments --- about Joanne and her journal.

After the visit in Auckland, it was apparent she couldn't go much further. The cruise schedule after Sydney was an overnight stop in the Philippines and then a long sail north to Shanghai in northern China. Then, the *South Seas Voyager* would slowly work down the coast to Hong Kong and Southeast Asia. I had been to Manila several times in years past on business, and while never having been to Shanghai, I didn't want Joanne to have to deal with the massive crowds at the airports and the general confusion of these major Asian cities.

She was failing quickly now. Sydney would be our last port of call.

When we returned to the ship in Lyttelton, I advised the concierge that we would be getting off in Sydney and asked him to please make arrangements for our flight back to North Carolina. Once again, I can't say enough about Regent Seven Seas Cruises. They advised that our flight would be arranged and the tickets would be ready when we departed. Further, we were not to worry about packing our luggage; they would do that for us and send it directly to our home.

We did take an additional two days in Australia to visit the Blue Mountains, which was something that was important to Joanne. They are a series of low mountain ridges --- much like our own Blue Ridge Mountains in North Carolina --- only an hour or so north of Sydney. The cruise line provided a car and driver, and we spent the night at the Lilianfels Spa in Katoomba. The Blue Mountains are famous for their eucalyptus trees that give off a blue or greenish-blue haze. I can say that only from the travel brochures because it was too foggy to see the view from our hotel.

I spent most of the day just looking out of the hotel window thinking about all of the things we had done, places we had been, and people we had met. I knew it was the last time we could discover new things together. She slept most of the time, but it didn't really matter. It was something Joanne wanted to do --- and we did it.

The driver came back for us the next day and we checked into a boutique hotel in Sydney to be ready for our flight home the next morning. Joanne was rested by then and we took a slow walk along the park across from our hotel. We came to a large church where we heard an organ playing but there didn't appear to be any other people around. We slipped into the back of the church to find only the organist practicing for the Easter service that was coming up in a few weeks.

It was the Cathedral of the Church of England in Sydney and it was just the two of us and the organist. His practice went on for almost an hour before he saw us sitting in the back of this magnificent cathedral. He stopped to say hello and welcomed us to come back for Easter. If only we could have.

It was a long flight home. In business class on Air New Zealand, the trip was better than I could have hoped for. After a plane change in Los Angeles and then another in Atlanta, we arrived home in North Carolina to find her friends waiting for us. Karen came several times each day and was a great comfort, not only for Joanne but for me as well. Melinda, our dear neighbor, also came everyday to work with Joanne as they made costume jewelry together. They would spread out their multi-colored beads on the dining room table to make outrageous combinations of bracelets and necklaces --- but they mostly talked and laughed together. When Joanne became too weak to even sit at the table, Melinda still came and sat cross legged on her bed with the beads spread out everywhere and they "worked" and laughed and laughed. There has never been a better friend than Melinda.

Betty and Carol and others came each day to help and visit. Joanne's sister Kathy, who lived and worked in Charlotte at that time, visited on the weekends. Her mother, at ninety-nine years old and living in a local retirement community, came only once during this period. She couldn't face the thought of her daughter dying --- it was just too much for her. She passed away a few months later, just a few days short of her one hundredth birthday.

On Dr. Radford's recommendation, I contacted our local hospice facility. Four Season's Hospice in Flat Rock is one of the great organizations in our area and provides a comfortable place for the terminally ill. Even thought they have a very caring staff and a wonderful facility, Joanne wanted to stay at home as long as she could. So with the help of the Four Seasons Hospice-At-Home program, and her two special nurses, Leann and Deanne, everything was done to make her comfortable at home.

During her last week, Mrs. Green, Deanne's mother, who was a retired CNA, was here from day light till dark just in case she could help and was needed. In that short time, we came to love Mrs. Green. She took such loving care of my dear Joanne and I'll never forget her.

The night before Joanne died, I sat in a recliner chair by her bed. In the darkness, my mind went back to all of the good times we had had together. She was sleeping peacefully, and her breathing was quite low. Suddenly she tried to get up and said softly, "I have to go now --- please help me."

I was surprised. She had said nothing all day. I leaned close to her and whispered, "Where do you want to go? Can I help you to the bathroom?"

She shook her head, settled back in her bed, and closed her eyes.

This happened several more times during the night, and just before daylight she asked, "I have to go now. When is Drew coming?" I said, "He'll be here this afternoon --- just as soon as he finishes his classes. It will be near the end of the day."

She drifted off to sleep again and those were her last words. She slept quietly all day.

Drew, a college professor, was living in Birmingham, Alabama. He had made the six-hour drive to our home in North Carolina several times during this final stage of Joanne's life. His time with Joanne had kept her going. She loved him as her own son. During a visit a few weeks earlier, she was happily showing Drew pictures on her camera from our last cruise. She lost her balance and fell over a small brass chest in our bedroom, cutting a large gash in her leg. We were off to the emergency room. When we returned home, I believe Drew was more upset by it all than Joanne, who was still excited to share her pictures.

When Drew arrived around 5:30 that evening, we visited for a few minutes and then we went to the bedroom to see Joanne. She was still sleeping and had not moved all day --- just quietly sleeping and waiting.

He sat down beside her on the bed, took her hand and began to talk with her as I left the room.

I went to the kitchen to begin dinner for the two of us --- probably another chicken pot pie out of the freezer. I opened a bottle of his favorite red wine. After about an hour, he came into the kitchen and said, "Dad, I was just sitting there holding her hand. She smiled and now I think she is gone."

It was seven o'clock on March 31st.

And this is where the story began.

CHAPTER

31

LATER IN THE MORNING OF APRIL 1, 2009

Drew looked at me and repeated, "What do you mean about the black pearl necklace?"

So I told him this story.

"Dad, could this be just an amazing coincidence? Or --- it's April 1st --- could this be some kind of cruel joke? How could this have happened --- half way around the world, the pearls being returned at the very same time Joanne died? How could this be possible?"

It had come to me as clear as a church bell. When the small box with the necklace was left at the front desk in the hotel lobby, there was a simple hand written note.

"Please forgive me."

I put my arm around Drew's shoulder, "God didn't want Joanne to arrive in heaven without knowing about her black pearl necklace. She waited for you --- and the black pearls. It may be the mystical power of the black pearls that they were returned but now they will be her lasting legacy for Mae."

Then I added, "I don't really know; however, if you truly believe in the grace of God, everything is possible. It is just as simple as that."

EPILOGUE

A few weeks later, we had a celebration of Joanne's life in Kenmure, the golf community in Flat Rock, North Carolina where I live. Hunter Huckabay, our long time friend and Episcopal Priest, provided the eulogy at the service. With his permission, the order of service follows as a fitting final summary of the remarkable life of Joanne Jones.

A Celebration of the Life of Joanne Davis Jones

April 21, 2009

Church of St. John in the Wilderness—
Flat Rock, North Carolina
First Reading—Ecclesiastes 3:1-13, 9:9
Gospel Reading—John 14:1-6a

We are here today to celebrate Joanne's remarkable life, and what a life it is! That is what she wanted, and as we all know, she was pretty good at making things happen the way she wanted.
  Ever since all of us began to gather in this beautiful place, we have all been telling and sharing stories about Joanne. I would encourage you to continue to tell those wonderful stories about her, because as we do, we help to keep her memory alive in our hearts. Prestine and I first met Joanne in Lafayette, Louisiana. We had

known Ken and had been friends for a long time. We had been with him through the death of his first wife, Jenny. We had seen his boys grow up and knew each of them. We had shared a lot of experiences with him.

One day Ken called and said, "I have someone I want you to meet". Something about the way he said that told us that this was someone special—and how special she was and is. We loved Joanne right away. She was gorgeous, fun, intelligent, and had a wonderful sense of humor and enthusiasm. We were not surprised and were in fact delighted to hear that they were planning a wedding.

I was honored to have the privilege of blessing their marriage. Our friendship deepened, and we enjoyed every minute of it. We visited Ken and Joanne in Maine and in Flat Rock. We celebrated with them at Andrew and Jean's wedding, and were there through the sad events of Stuart's death. We shared and experienced good times and painful times. Ken and Joanne were a wonderful source of strength and support and love to each other. In the words of the wedding service, their mutual affection and support led them to reach out in love and concern for those around them. Every person here has been touched by their genuine care, concern, and generosity. We have all seen the leadership and the positive impact that Joanne and Ken have had on every community in which they lived.

Prestine and I love to travel, and have been fortunate enough to be able to do a fair amount of it. Joanne always did our travel arrangements with great energy and joy, and they were unfailingly perfect in every detail. She always seemed to be as excited about our trips as we were, and her enthusiasm was contagious. She charmed the concierges in every hotel in which we stayed, so that we were received and treated like celebrities. She constantly pushed us to be more luxurious in our planning, and reminded us with regularity, "Life is not a dress rehearsal!"

Joanne told me once that she had two regrets about her life.

One was that she never had a chance to dance with the Rockettes and the other was that she never was licensed as a jet pilot. What a combination—what a remarkable human being! Those two regrets speak volumes about her life.

She also said that she had two last wishes. She wanted to experience one more football season and she wanted to go on the cruise around the world. Joanne was able to fulfill both of those wishes, and her daily journals from aboard ship brightened all our lives, even as we marveled at her courage and determination to live life to the fullest. Ken had made arrangements so that Joanne could bring all of the clothes she wanted, and I have no doubt that she was easily the best dressed person on the ship. In one of her journal messages she summed it up, "We are blissfully happy! Life is good!"

When Joanne and Ken returned from the cruise, her condition had deteriorated and it was clear that her life was nearing the end. Prestine and I came for a last visit just a few days before she died. We had some heartfelt talks, we laughed and we cried together.

What assurances does our faith give us about Joanne now? First, we are assured and I firmly believe that she has been welcomed into the arms of our merciful and loving God. She is in God's hands, free of all pain and stress; and she is experiencing a greater joy and peace than she has ever known.

Another assurance we have is that it is all right to grieve. While it is true that Joanne is in a better place, it is also true that we miss her in this life. We sometimes get the mistaken idea that it is selfish to grieve for someone we love who has died, because they are free of suffering now and in a better place, and we should be happy for them. While we are glad that she is in a better place, and no one of us would want Joanne to return to the pain and stress of her last days, still we are saddened that she is gone from this life. There is nothing selfish about grieving the death of someone we love—nor does our grief indicate a lack of faith. St. Paul speaks directly to this in his first letter to the Thessalonians.

(I Thessalonians 4:13-18) He writes, "We would not have you ignorant, friends, concerning those who are asleep (died), that you may not grieve as others do who have no hope."

It is important to note here, I believe, that Paul does not say that we should not grieve. We grieve, but we grieve with hope. We grieve with the "sure and certain hope of the resurrection to eternal life" *(Prayer Book, p. 485)* That brings us to the final assurance that our faith brings us—the assurance of life beyond this world. We will see Joanne again and will be with her in eternal life. We do not know all of the details, but in the reading from the Gospel of John *(John 14:1-6a)*, our Lord assures us that He is going to prepare a place for us—and He will bring us there to be with Him--and that is enough.

Joanne once said to me, "I don't consider myself particularly religious, but I do have a spiritual heart and I live by it." One of our prayers used to bless the bread and wine of Holy Communion speaks of "those whose faith is known to God alone". *(Eucharistic Prayer D page 375 of the Prayer Book).* I believe Joanne was one of those people, and God knows her heart and loves her.

I do know this; Joanne requested and received anointing in the Name of the Father, Son and Holy Spirit. Here are the words of the anointing prayer, "I anoint you with oil, and lay my hands upon you in the Name of the Father and of the Son, and of the Holy Spirit, beseeching the mercy of our Lord Jesus Christ, that all your pain and sickness being put to flight, the blessing of health may be restored to you." With those words, the Sign of the Cross is made on the forehead of the person receiving anointing—just as it is in baptism. Joanne may be one, whose faith is fully known to God alone, but her faith is there, and God knows her and loves her.

It has been said, and I cannot remember where this comes from, "Out of His love, God has created each of us as a unique human being. We please God most by being fully the person He created us to be and by living each day of our lives as fully as possible." Joanne did that as well as anyone I have ever known.

She lived every day of her life as fully as possible, and I am sure God is well pleased with her.

As Prestine and I were preparing to leave after our last visit to Flat Rock, Joanne said, "Before you go, I have to show you my wigs." She then insisted on getting out of bed and putting on what I called a sassy wig show. She modeled each one of her wigs—striking a classic pose or two with each one—delighting all three of us, looking absolutely beautiful and having a grand time. It is one of my warmest and fondest memories.

All of us enjoyed and were amazed by her journals from the Regent 7 Cruise. In her final entry, she quotes the lyrics of a favorite song, and declares them to be her mantra. "If you have the chance to sit out or dance, I hope you dance." She concludes her journal by saying, "My friends, we have danced!"

Yes, Joanne, you have danced, and you will always dance in our hearts until we all dance together with you in Heaven.

AMEN

A Final Thought

MAY 26, 2017

After Joanne passed away in 2009, through the grace of God and Father Alex Viola, I met Sandy Hunter, who was the director of Christian Education at our small Episcopal church in Flat Rock, North Carolina. We attended the Wednesday night summer reading programs. In 2010, the featured book was *A Grief Observed* by C.S. Lewis, a memoir about the death of his wife and how he dealt with the loss. While I knew of Lewis from his reputation as a provocative writer, this was my first real exposure to him. It was an important book to me. During these programs, there was also a pot luck dinner involved, but in deference to my single status, Father Alex excused me from doing any cooking.

At the end of the summer, a season of free home-cooked meals, I asked Sandy, whom I had sat with during the programs, "Now that this is over, what are we going to do for dinner next Wednesday night?"

She was surprised. After a pause, she said, "Well, I guess I could fix dinner at my house." One thing led to another, and after a year or so, we decided to get married and Father Alex officiated at the service.

Many years earlier, my oldest son Kevin and his wife Linda

moved from Seattle to the Texas Hill Country and bought a home in Wimberley, just a few miles south and west of Austin. More recently, Drew and Jean and their three children relocated from Birmingham to Austin to be near the University of Texas, where he is a college professor. My two sons live only about thirty miles apart now.

For the past several years, Sandy and I have made trips to Austin for holidays and family occasions. In 2017, three special events came together at the same time: Mae was home from college in Colorado for her twenty-first birthday, Drew and Jean's twin boys, Christopher and Stuart, were graduating with honors from Saint Andrew's Episcopal High School, and Kevin's beautiful youngest daughter Lily was getting married. All great reasons for a family celebration.

Jean, as she often does, hosted a dinner party at their house for our family and several of their friends. Since this was a special evening, we were all a little more dressed than usual for these family affairs. It was a grand evening and a great time was had by all.

As Sandy and I were leaving to go back to our hotel, Mae came over to me, "Grandpa, did you notice that I'm wearing Joanne's black pearl necklace?"

I took her hand and gave her a hug.

"Yes, I did. They look lovely on you." After a pause, I added, "I know Joanne is looking down from heaven with her big smile --- and you have made us both very happy tonight."

Joanne's legacy lives on.

A Personal Reflection

Joanne was a huge Anglophile. She loved everything about England and we spent many happy hours in London and the English countryside. When in London, we always stayed at the Connaught Hotel in the Mayfair District and walked the area parks and squares. After she died, I put a small medallion on a park bench in Berkeley Square so she would always be there. As I wrote this memoir, each time I closed my eyes, I heard this song.

> *That certain night, the night we met,*
>   *There was magic abroad in the air.*
> *There were angels dining at the Ritz*
>   *And a nightingale sang in Berkeley Square.*
>
> *I may be right, I may be wrong,*
>   *But I'm perfectly willing to swear.*
> *That when you turned and smiled at me,*
>   *A nightingale sang in Berkeley Square.*

These are the first eight lines of the beautiful song written by Eric Maschwitz in 1939. It was made famous by Vera Lynn during the early part of World War II as many American GIs fell in love for the first time with a pretty young girl from London Town.

"A Nightingale Sang in Berkeley Square" has been recorded by dozens of artists over the years and remains one of my favorite songs.

I'll never forget these lovely words ... a nightingale indeed.

Special Thanks

I never really understood what editing was all about until I started writing these books. I have imposed on several of my friends by asking them to help me with this process. It is amazing that you can look at something you have written --- or you think you have written --- and your mind makes the corrections even if your eyes don't see the words in the same way. This applies to typographical errors, grammar and sentence structure.

So here is a thank you to all who have helped --- and a special thanks to Ed and Ann Destremps, old friends who have been an enormous help to me in editing *"Letters from the Skeleton Coast"* and now *"The Black Pearl Necklace."*

Just One More Thought

In case you haven't read my first book, *Letters from the Skeleton Coast,* it is a true story that begins in 1942 when the *Dunedin Star* runs aground on the desolate coast of Southwest Africa while carrying supplies and ammunition to Egypt. Among the passengers is Alison Habib, a young Scottish woman traveling from England to Cairo with her Egyptian doctor husband and their eighteen-month-old daughter, Caroline. The events that followed become a memoir in 2003 as my wife, Joanne, and I connect an old-fashioned love story that remained a secret for more than sixty over years. The book was published by Lulu Press in April, 2017; the prologue and the first two chapters are reprinted here.

LETTERS FROM THE SKELETON COAST

Prologue

November 29, 1942

"I just don't like the way she feels." First Officer Williamson broke the silence in the wheelhouse of the *Dunedin Star,* where he and two other officers were on duty for the night watch. He drummed his fingers on the wheel before looking over to the second officer. "Here, you take her for a while and see what you think."

Williamson stepped away so the second officer could take the wheel and turned to the navigator, who was making his first trip on the *Dunedin Star.* "How long are we to stay on this course?"

The young officer replied, "Sir, it's only 2230. The way I have it plotted, we stay on this heading for another twenty-five minutes."

Williamson walked over to the navigation table. "How in the hell can that be?" It looks like it's getting brighter to port. Let me look at that chart."

Shaking his head, Williamson picked up the intercom, keyed the mike, and said, "Captain O'Brien, please come to the bridge." Just as he slipped the intercom back into place, the ship shuddered, and there was a low grinding sound that filled the wheelhouse.

"Damn!" Williamson muttered, knowing this could mean one of two things, neither of them good. The *Dunedin Star* had hit something in the open sea; maybe a submerged object like a

German submarine, or the ship was off course and had hit a reef not shown on the chart.

Timothy O'Brien, who had just finished dinner and was making his final entries in the ship's log for November 29, quickly climbed the stairs into the wheelhouse.

"What the hell was that?" O'Brien barked.

"I don't know, Captain, but it's getting brighter to port, and I think I see a line that may be the surf."

O'Brien, one of the most experienced senior officers in the Blue Star fleet, turned to the officer at the wheel. "Reduce power to fifty percent and change our course ninety degrees to starboard!" The new course would take the *Dunedin Star* away from the coast of Africa.

O'Brien snapped to the navigator, "Confirm our position."

The young navigator paused for a moment before responding. "Sir, based on our dead reckoning position, I think we are at eighteen degrees, thirteen minutes south latitude and seventeen degrees, fifty-five minutes east longitude. That's twelve miles from Cape Frio on the coast of southwest Africa."

"Damn it, son, don't tell me where you think we are. Tell me where we are!"

O'Brien checked the ship's position the navigator had marked on the chart. If this was correct, the ship would be miles west of the nearest landfall. "This can't be," O'Brien stated. "It's getting brighter because that's the surf piling up on the shore."

An alarm bell sounded, and an engineer in the machinery room reported, "We are taking on water, and the pumps are not able to keep up. There appears to be a big cut in the hull between the third and fourth bulkhead, and the water is already up to the floor plates."

O'Brien quickly considered his options. If he continued on the new course due west, the ship could sink in the deep water of the South Atlantic, with the possible loss of everyone on board. His other choice was to change heading and attempt to beach the ship on what the chart called the Skeleton Coast.

"Change course one hundred and eighty degrees to port and full speed ahead." He picked up the intercom and keyed the radio operator. "This is Capitan O'Brien. Send an SOS to anyone within radio range. Tell them we are taking on water and this is a mayday call."

O'Brien turned and put his hand on the shoulder of the second officer. "I'll take the wheel now." Then, looking directly at Williamson, "Keith, prepare the passengers and crew to abandon ship."

1

April 27, 2015

I had read this tattered little blue book about the demise of the *Dunedin Star* many times over the past dozen years. Why was I reading it again tonight? I paused, marked the page, and put it on the table next to my chair in exchange for a glass of red wine. Earlier in the evening, I had opened a prized bottle of Cabernet, which I had saved for a special occasion. There was really nothing special about tonight; it was just another Sunday evening at home. Or was it? I had just returned earlier in the afternoon from a writers' retreat after a weekend in the Western Carolina Mountains and was in an unusually reflective mood.

Maybe it was the warm feeling you get from a really good vintage French red, or perhaps just that last line I had read in the book. Whatever it was, those words—"abandon ship"—sent my mind reeling. The *Dunedin Star* had been underway from Liverpool for twenty-three days when the captain issued those orders: two words that send fear into the hearts of anyone who has ever gone to sea.

I was thinking of Alison and what must have been in her mind. Day after day of gray seas and overcast skies, she was lonely, confused, and now threatened by the world around her. What was she doing on this ship with people she did not know and on the way to a life she did not understand and had no reference for? Just twenty-two years old, she was traveling with her eighteen-month-old daughter and her middle-aged Egyptian husband to Cairo, nearly halfway around the world from her farm life on the coast of northern Scotland.

Then my thoughts went to Joanne, lovely and sophisticated, who had traveled most everywhere. First with Pan American Airways as a flight attendant, then with an international oil company, and later as my wife, she thrived on the unknown and always handled new situations with confidence and optimism. Born in San Francisco into a life of abundance, with such different backgrounds, how did she and Alison become best of friends?

And how did this little blue book, written about events that took place off the coast of Africa during World War II, lead to a private conversation sixty years later when these two remarkable women shared a secret that changed our lives forever?

I shook my head, took another sip of that deep blackberry flavor of the 1990 Chateau Rothschild, and wondered the odds—maybe one in a million or more—that this little blue book and the stories that followed would come into my possession and to my reading table tonight.

I saw it more clearly than ever before; there are really two love stories here. They are real, intense, and personal; and I'm the only one who knows.

So why did I go to the Writers' High Retreat in the first place, if I had not wanted to share these stories with others? I had never written anything before, other than business reports, so could I really do justice to the events and the people involved? Was it even my right to try?

I swirled the wine, looking into that dark-ruby color as my thoughts came together. I closed my eyes. "I'm eighty-three years old, and if I don't tell this story now, it will be lost forever."

In that moment of clarity, I refilled my glass, walked down the hall into my cluttered office, turned on the computer, and began to write.

2

May 25, 2003

As we flew over the barren landscape, I saw the green belt that marked the flood zone for the Nile and knew we would soon be approaching the three pyramids on the outskirts of Cairo, where we would touch down. My business partner, Omar Ryad; my wife, Joanne; and I had spent the day visiting new helicopter-maintenance bases near the Red Sea.

Joanne loved to fly and had been excited about making this trip, but the long day and steady beat of the rotor blades had lulled her to sleep. I stole a glance and shook my head. Even after a day in the desert and a long ride in a cramped helicopter, she looked relaxed and beautiful. The bulky headset had mussed her blonde hair, and a few strands fell across her cheek. I hated to disturb her, but I knew she'd be upset if I didn't. I pushed the talk button on my headset. "Joanne, you don't want to miss the sunset over the Nile and Giza. We may never get a chance to see this again."

She opened her eyes and smiled at me. She didn't turn on her talk button, but I knew what she was saying. "Oh thanks, honey. I don't want to miss anything." She reached over and gave my hand a little squeeze before rearranging herself so she could gaze out the window.

Beneath us, the early-evening lights of Cairo flickered for miles. The pilot began a slow descent to a small landing area near the pyramids as the throng of tourists and postcard vendors quickly moved away from the downwash of the mammoth rotor blades.

Our helicopter, a twin-engine Bell 212 painted red and white with the letters "EAS" in black on the tail boom, was one of my company's workhorses. Energy Aviation Service's fleet of fifty aircraft was typically used to transport a dozen oil workers to offshore drilling rigs, but today it was carrying just the three of us and the flight crew. The slight jarring of the landing also woke Omar, who was the EAS general manager and our host for the trip.

As the blades slowed to an idle position, the young copilot stepped down from the left-front seat and opened the sliding exit door. Getting out of the 212's passenger cabin was awkward at best, so EAS had a special three-step ladder made for VIP flights, but it still required a crewman to give the passengers a hand. We gave him our headsets and life jackets, I thanked him for another smooth flight, and Joanne gave him her customary hug.

The tourists and vendors had gathered near our waiting limousine, wanting to see if we were important. Even though she'd been asleep minutes earlier, Joanne looked wide awake and waved to the crowd. I smiled at her and winked at Omar. "She always likes to arrive in style."

We slipped inside the limo, sinking into the plush leather seats as our driver eased the vehicle into the chaotic traffic that is Cairo at night.

During the twenty-minute drive to the Nile Hilton, the three of us could finally stretch our legs and enjoy the quiet. We'd known each other so long the silence was a comfortable one. Omar had been both friend and business partner for years, and we'd spent many hours together building our business in Egypt. In his younger days, he'd been a fighter pilot and was regarded as the only true Egyptian hero in the 1973 war with Israel, where he shot down the one aircraft lost in that seven-day conflict. He was later shot down himself and, as a result of the accident, had a slight limp, but he still carried himself with a military bearing. According to my wife, he was tall, dark, and quite handsome. Joanne told me more than once that Omar reminded her of the movie star Omar Sharif.

"Ken, I know it's been a long day and we're all tired, but since this is your last night here, Caroline has planned dinner at our apartment so Alison can see Joanne again."

"How is my dear Alison?" Joanne asked. She adored Omar's mother-in-law and considered her one of her best friends.

Omar sighed before responding. "She hasn't been doing well. She's eighty-three now, and we've moved her into our apartment."

"Oh, I'm sorry to hear that. I know Caroline must be relieved to have her at home so she can keep an eye on her."

He laughed. "Well, you know how it is with Caroline and Alison. They always love each other, but they don't always get along."

That made us all laugh. It was true. Caroline was a strong woman, successful in a culture that often didn't support those roles for women. Still, Alison, petite in stature, was a strong woman herself, although much softer spoken.

"I can't wait to see Alison," Joanne said. "It's been almost a year since our last visit."

Omar smiled. "Joanne, you have no idea how excited she is. She's been talking about this visit for months and about seeing you again."

Joanne returned the smile. "She's a dear woman who has had a remarkable life."

"You've had a pretty remarkable life yourself," I teased.

Joanne gave me a quick glance. "Alison has shared so many

stories with me over the years, but she is still a very private person and a little shy."

Omar nodded. "We've told Alison that Ken is planning to retire, so she knows this might be her last chance to see her beloved Joanne."

KENMURE FIGHTS CANCER

Joanne was one of the founders of our community program that is now called Kenmure Fights Cancer. In 2005, along with several others, she organized a Susan G. Komen, "Rally for a Cure." They raised $40,000 that first year for national cancer research through a golf and tennis tournament and a gala celebration dinner at the Kenmure County Club. It was a big success.

Over the years, the baton has been passed to a talented group of residents who volunteer their time and expertise on a year around basis. The Kenmure Fights Cancer is now a donor advised fund of the Community Foundation of Henderson County. In recent years, more than $300,000 has been gifted to the cancer centers of Pardee Hospital and Park Ridge Health for equipment and technology in the realm of patient care.

In recognition of the work being done by the many volunteers here in the beautiful mountains of Western North Carolina, any profits from the sale of this book will be given to Kenmure Fights Cancer. I hope you will encourage your friends and neighbors to support their good work by purchasing a copy of *The Black Pearl Necklace*, which is now available online or at book stores everywhere. For further information on Kenmure Fights Cancer, go to www.KenmureFightsCancer.org or contact the Community Foundation of Henderson County at (828) 697-6224 or info@CFHCforever.org.

NOTE

The cover photograph for the book was taken at daybreak in the islands of the South Pacific as we searched for Joanne's black pearl necklace.

The inset photograph on the back cover was taken from the small pub in Lyttelton, New Zealand as we waited to return to the *South Seas Voyager* shown in the background.

Made in the USA
Coppell, TX
15 September 2023